Listen to Your ANIMALS

They Know More Than You Think

Listen to Your ANIMALS

They Know More Than You Think

Karen Wickerson, M.A., H.T.A.C.P.,
Animal Telepath

Listen to Your Animals: They Know More Than You Think
Published by KWET Media
Vancouver, BC, Canada

Disclaimer: The content of this book and information being provided does not replace, overlook, or disregard traditional veterinary healthcare. My role as an animal communicator and telepath is not to diagnose, treat, or prescribe medications. Anything inside these pages regarding an animal's physical, mental, or emotional well-being is solely from their point of view and does not replace the medical opinion of your licensed veterinarian. For traditional medical care or for questions concerning specific illnesses, please consult your licensed veterinarian. For full transparency, the names of the animals and their owners who appear within these pages have provided consent. If consent has not been provided, the names have been omitted or changed to protect their identities and privacy.

Definitions are resourced from the Cambridge Dictionary, Merriam-Webster Dictionary, Encyclopedia Britannica, and Collins Dictionary and have been reconfigured to suit the author's needs.

WICKERSON, KAREN, Author
LISTEN TO YOUR ANIMALS
KAREN WICKERSON

ISBN: 978-1-0690651-0-0, 978-1-0690651-1-7 (paperback)
ISBN: 978-1-0690651-2-4 (hardcover)
ISBN: 978-1-0690651-3-1(digital)

BODY, MIND & SPIRIT / Afterlife & Reincarnation
FAMILY & RELATIONSHIPS / Death, Grief, Bereavement
PETS / Essays & Narratives
BODY, MIND & SPIRIT / Channeling & Mediumship

Editing: Alyssa Berthiaumen (thewriteplacerighttime.com)
Editing: Lisa Shrewsberry (shrewsberry5live@gmail.com)
Interior & E-book Design: Amit Dey (amitdey2528@gmail.com)
Publishing Management: Susie Schaefer (FinishTheBookPublishing.com)

QUANTITY PURCHASES: Schools, companies, professional groups, clubs, and other organizations may qualify for special terms when ordering quantities of this title. For information, email kwetmedia@shaw.ca

DEDICATION

This book is dedicated to Divine Creator and all the animals I've ever had the honor of working with and talking to. Without the skills and gifts that were bestowed upon me by Divine Creator, I would not have the incredible privilege and opportunity to serve the animal kingdom.

TABLE OF CONTENTS

*"Goodbyes are only for those who love with their eyes,
because for those who love with heart and soul there is
no such thing as separation."*

—Rumi

OPENING THE CHANNEL

I was not your typical girl who liked to play with and dress up her dolls. In fact, I left that to my younger sister, Ainsley. I was the girl who kept her dolls at bay, untouched, and couldn't be bothered to play with them. Mine were in pristine condition, however, Ainsley's always had the newest "haircut," fashionwear and crayon "makeup" all over their faces. I was the kind of girl that had stuffed animals all around me, especially bunnies. I played with those animals, I loved those animals, and I made sure they were well "fed," "watered," played with and "safe." Of course, a few of them had "war wounds" with stitches around their eyes, ears, legs, and bellies. In my little girl's mind, we went on so many adventures and safaris. They were my "kids", and I loved them to bits.

These animals were a comfort to me. I believed they kept me safe, protected, and surrounded me with love. *The Velveteen Rabbit* comes to mind. As a little girl, I truly believed my stuffed animals were real. Way before the movie *Toy Story* came out, I always believed that my stuffed animals would come to life and play with one another when I wasn't home or when I was deep asleep.

Along with my stuffed animals, the wallpaper in my room alongside my bed had ABCs with characters such as teddy bears, Raggedy Anne and Andy, and a rocking horse. When I couldn't fall asleep, I would look up onto the wallpaper and imagine Raggedy Anne and Andy telling tales to the teddy bears and rocking horses about all the adventures they'd been on that day. I would imagine that rocking horse popping off the wallpaper, jumping on its back, and taking off rocking away through the window and into the night's sky towards my own adventures. Unfortunately, I don't remember those adventures or faraway places the rocking horse and I went on because that's when I would finally fall asleep. My stuffies were the first interactions I'd have with animals.

I knew that deep within something was telling me I needed to have live animals in my life whether they belonged to myself or family members, or by becoming a veterinarian. Yup, I always wanted to be a veterinarian so I could heal them. I completely disregarded the fact that I'm fully allergic to all animals and I have chronic asthma. It didn't matter to me; I just knew I needed them in my life in one way or another. Never did I ever imagine that throughout my lifetime, I would have fish, cats, hamsters, and rabbits and even become an animal communicator and animal energy worker.

My deep connection with *living* animals came in the summer of 1971, in Montreal, Quebec. This was one of those critical life moments when nothing will ever be the same even though I didn't have the words to express it at the time. It's only in looking back that I recognize it was the first tap, the first nudge from Source of what my purpose on this earth would be.

I was at a farm attending a birthday party. I remember being shy as I didn't know anybody but also excited at the same time because hey, it was a birthday party and who doesn't love colored balloons, streamers, games, presents and cake?!? The biggest surprise, however, was the moment this huge creature made an appearance. The excitement grew within me with each passing second; the desire of being on that horse was more than I could bear. I just knew with every fiber of my being that I needed a chance to sit on its back.

I could hardly wait for my turn; I just wanted to get on that horse. I was willing to push my way through the lineup of kids all waiting turns but, of course, my mum had to remind me that I had to wait my turn. So I did, but each minute I had to wait for my turn to get on that incredible, gigantic creature just to walk around the paddock felt like an eternity.

By the time I was the next in line, I could barely contain myself from the anticipation and excitement. Then it was my turn.

Still in my little red and blue bikini, I was picked up by the hostess of the party and placed on the back of this incredibly beautiful horse. As soon as I sat on him, I felt like I was home; in the imagination of a three-year-old, I believed I could live on him for the rest of my life. I didn't ever want to get down. I didn't care that it was a sunny, hot day and the leather of the saddle was sticking to the back of my legs and getting uncomfortable. Plus, I was way too small for the saddle, and I didn't care that my little hands were too small to pick up the reins; I just held onto the saddle's pommel.

Needless to say, it was a seminal moment in my life—the connection we shared was undeniable. I instantly fell in love with not only this horse but with all horses. At some level, I knew I had to have horses in my life one way or another. The love I felt for this horse was bigger than my little body could contain. No words were spoken between us, but my heart sang with joy. I felt his care, as he knew his job (responsibility), and the energy that transmitted between the two of us was through physical sensations. I knew immediately that I was safe on this majestic being. This was the beginning of my ability to connect to and communicate with animals.

Was this a fluke? Was this a one-off? Nope, not even in the slightest. I just didn't know it way back then.

Even though I wasn't surrounded by animals in my younger years, every time I encountered a dog or cat, they'd make themselves known to me and their humans would say: "Wow, they've never done that before! They usually run away when people come over." I didn't think anything of it at the time; I was just being myself. The majority of my interactions with animals resulted in an immediate connection and my immediately knowing them, even if it was the first time we had met. No words were passed, just physical and emotional sensations. Most of the time, I didn't know what it meant, I just knew I had an undeniable connection with animals.

Remember, this was back in the 1970s when there was little understanding about psychic abilities/clairsentience. Up until this point, I honestly thought it was normal for people to be connected on so deep a level with the animals they encountered. However, into my preteens and early teens, I realized this wasn't true. My friends weren't that way, and most adults weren't either.

Eventually, I came to shut down this connection because I wanted to fit in, to be understood, and to be liked by my friends and their parents—especially my friends' parents. They would call me "crazy Karen" when I would spontaneously tell them what their animal was thinking–and while I can't remember specific instances that elicited their calling me this, that hardly matters. What I know is that this was the name they gave me, and it didn't feel good. I started to believe there was something wrong with me, so I stopped paying attention to the animals; I loved them, but I didn't want to feel them anymore. It wasn't really a conscious decision at that age. You just know that something is different from everyone else and whatever it is, you begin to shut it down so it doesn't disrupt your life.

It wasn't until my mid-teens when I was able to start seeing energy—sort of like the heat thermals off a hot road on a sunny day—emanating from plants and grass. I didn't quite understand what it was, but I chose not to shut it off. I instinctively knew that I needed to keep an open mind and just go with the flow and figure out what it all meant. Over the course of my teen years, my family adopted three cats, I became an equestrian, and my connection, again, was undeniable.

In my late twenties, it was my mother who suggested I take Healing Touch classes out of Langara College in Vancouver, Canada. (We had moved from Montreal to Toronto when I was four, and then I moved to Vancouver at 28.) At that point in time, she had been hearing me talk about seeing energies for roughly eleven years. I don't remember exactly what I had shared at that time in my life, but it prompted my mum to suggest the classes, as she happened to have a friend whose daughter was taking them, too, around that time.

After looking into the classes and talking with her more about it, it was clear to me that I didn't know what seeing and feeling energy was all about and what it meant, or what I could do with it. The instructors at Langara were just the beginning of my path that led me to where I am today with animal communication. It gave me the foundation and fundamentals of how energy works, and how it can help to facilitate healing within the body.

During this time, I also completed my undergraduate and masters level degrees in counseling and was hired by a local Family Services agency in my community to work as a Family Clinical Counselor which I did for eleven years. This included providing services to families who were at risk of having their children removed from the family due to addiction, mental health issues, abuse, or neglect. Some families needed guidance, direction, and overall support in becoming higher-functioning parents to their children. I enjoyed the work I was doing with the families, and I had the honor of working with over 200 families in my community over those eleven years. For most of the time, I enjoyed it. My fellow team members were incredibly supportive of one another, helped through the difficult times, through accomplishments, successes, and challenges. It was the most difficult, challenging, and rewarding time in my professional counseling career. However, it took a toll on my physical, mental, and emotional health.

During my eighth year at the family agency in 2012, I could see the writing on the wall. I sensed within myself that I needed to start the transition out of my clinical counseling job and into a different vocation.

In the three years between recognizing I needed to change vocations and leaving my work as a family counselor, my interest in healing touch for humans and animals piqued again when a good friend of mine, also named Karen, knew this and asked if I could alleviate some excruciating pain she'd been experiencing in her big toe. She could barely walk, had been living in pain for a few weeks, and needed some relief. I told her I only knew some basics but would review my materials from previous courses and would work on her toe. When we got together and I started applying the different healing touch techniques to her painful toe, she said she could feel relief and was surprised that by the end of our session her pain was virtually gone. She asked me if I could work on her daughter's horse, Gabby, whose behaviour was out of sorts.

Karen's family had been trying to sell Gabby, but this had proven unsuccessful. She couldn't quite describe the horse's behavior, but she said she just wasn't herself. Gabby wasn't training well and executing the jumps well, either. When I arrived at the barn to meet up with her horse, I slowly put my hands in her energy field and immediately felt an overwhelming sadness; tears started flowing down my cheeks. I was crying and yet I didn't understand what was happening, I just knew that it wasn't me who was sad. I wasn't upset, yet I was crying. It was an unsettling experience because how I was emotionally feeling—contentment and joy—was not congruent to the tears and heaviness I felt when I put my hands in Gabby's energy field. When I tuned into Gabby with my mind and heart, I immediately realized that it was Gabby who was shedding tears through me. My heart and mind's eye reached out to her heart and mind's eye to understand more about what happened and why there was the heaviness of sadness.

Gabby began to show me pictures of a baby foal who was around Gabby and then *poof* the foal was gone. The story continued and I was able to figure out that, in her mind, her foal was stolen from her by a human and she never saw her foal again. She never got to raise her foal, even though the foal was two years old when sold; she couldn't say goodbye to her, and she'd been grieving since then.

As I communicated Gabby's story to my friend and her daughter, they filled in the blanks. Gabby's baby had been sold and nobody told her that her baby was permanently going away! Also, what came up during our interaction was that Gabby no longer wanted to compete as a hunter/jumper or have someone older riding her. She wasn't enjoying herself. Through mental images, Gabby had shown me little children, youngsters around the ages of five to eleven, teaching them how to ride at a beginner level. Gabby wanted to belong to a family, but specifically she longed to be with a little girl who could grow up learning how to ride her.

After all this information was communicated, my friend and her daughter apologized to Gabby for her experience of having her foal taken away and their ignorance of her desires to be ridden by a younger girl and no longer wishing to be a hunter/jumper horse. There was a lot of compassion, empathy, and love flowing through the four of us. They made her a promise that they would find her a home where she would be happy, which they did within a week with a family who had a five-year-old girl; the girl wanted to learn how to ride horses. Later on, Gabby was sold as a school horse to help young children learn how to ride and, according to my friend's daughter, she's been very happy there ever since.

It was during this interaction with Gabby when I remembered I had always had the ability to talk with animals. It all came flooding back—the skill, the knowledge, the know-how, the memories of having conversations with animals while I was growing up. The floodgates opened and my abilities were turned on like a faucet. I had yet to learn how to turn my abilities "on" at will, but it was certainly an exciting experience whenever it happened.

Throughout 2012, I applied what I learned from my previous courses of Therapeutic Touch and Healing Touch for People to other horses, dogs, and cats. In late 2012, I discovered Healing Touch for Animals˚ and other certification programs.

While working as a Clinical Counselor with families in their homes, the one thing I noticed was that the adults tended to treat their animals a lot better than their own children! This was often a common thread from one family to another, and this realization influenced my decision about my next vocation.

I knew I still wanted to make a difference in people's lives, but I didn't want to work directly with people. I decided then I would take the courses from the Founder and Developer of Healing Touch for Animals˚ (HTA˚), Carol Komitor.

I don't believe in coincidences at all; I believe that Universal Source always guides me in the direction I need to go and, once again, that's what the Universe did for me. Carol was holding a lucky draw contest for Valentine's Day for a free Level 1 HTA˚ course, so I put my name in for the draw and, lo and behold, my name was picked! I was stunned—I never, ever, win through draws, ever! Winning that drawing was confirmation that HTA˚ was the way to go. This was going to be my Plan B—my backup plan—as my father calls it.

So, in April 2013, I flew to Calgary to take my Level 1 HTA˚ course. That was the beginning of my travels throughout North America to take all the HTA˚ course levels to become a certified HTA˚ practitioner. 2013 was a very busy year as I was also working full time and taking these classes. I was living, eating, and dreaming about HTA˚ and all the incredible animals I got to work with and help along the way. Carol became an incredible mentor to me, steering me, challenging me, and helping my abilities and skills to flourish.

In 2014, once all my levels were completed, Carol strongly encouraged me to complete my HTA* certification which took that full year. During this time, I also realized I couldn't continue working full time in counseling and part time with animals, so I decided to go part time in counseling to develop my energy therapy practice.

In August of 2015, after completing the requirements with my family's and Carol's encouragement and support, I received my certification in August 2015. In September, I gave a month's notice to my agency and notified them I was retiring from the counseling field altogether, and in October I left counseling for good.

A new level of my abilities opened to me in my mid-forties when I learned that I was able to communicate with animals who had died. An acquaintance asked if I was able to talk with animals who had passed away. I admitted I didn't know if I could, but I was willing to try even though I had never met her dog before. When I saw the picture of her dog, who had passed six months before, my voice immediately took on the characteristics of her dog, I felt my voice wanting to go deeper (but it couldn't), it took on a gruff sound and I immediately pictured in my mind's eye a dog who was dressed as a security guard. It was not at all what I was expecting; it was immediate. The words and pictures were clear, and he wanted his human to know that he had taken on the role of security of her family and home, and that he would always be there to protect them in spirit and not allow anything to happen to them, especially the children. A whole new world of animal communication opened to me and to my current and future clients.

It's this whole new world—communicating with spirits of animals and everything they've taught me about death and the afterlife—that I especially want to bring to you now through this book, though it won't be the only thing I share. There's plenty else to learn from animals about matters of life such as things regarding food, safety, and relationships. But the heart of this book and the thing I want you to walk away with the most is what I've come to know about death.

I realize death is a huge topic and my intention is to keep it strictly to the animals' experiences of the death journey as well as their experiences once they've transitioned out of their bodies.

When I first started on the animal communication journey of my career, I believed there was life after death. I wasn't sure how that'd look or how it worked, but I had an inner knowing that my soul would continue after it left my physical body. Do I believe that life is finite? With the physical body, yes. Once my physical body dies that's it. However, I always believed that my soul, my true essence, continues. I always saw my soul as taking up an adventure with a different body, different characteristics, and different personalities as it travels from one physical lifetime to another.

However, once I started to talk with animals and especially through my experiences with their dying and transition process, my understanding and perspective of death and dying, learning from them to applying it to my own reality now, has shifted immensely. Learning and hearing from the animals has given me a deeper understanding of death and dying, a greater sense of peace, a greater sense of ease of mind, knowing that life does carry on after our animals and we leave our bodies. I'm now sharing the gift of this knowledge and wisdom with you.

My want for the reader is to open their mindset (or belief system) and consider that death isn't as finite as we believe—that life continues beyond death. My intention for the reader is to have a peace of mind and heart when reading this book knowing their animal(s) is/are still alive; they are happy and not suffering in their physical body anymore.

Does this mean that our grief is any less when our animals die? Does it mean that we're not supposed to grieve? Does it mean that we shouldn't miss them once they leave their physical bodies? Absolutely not! We will grieve, we will miss them deeply, and we will find it heartbreaking to know we'll never feel their fur, feathers, scales, or fins ever again, never be able to smell them, to see them, to hear their sounds, barks, woofs, purrs, hisses, squeaks, or chirps. It's part of our human makeup—we'll miss them fiercely because they were a valued member of our family. They served us in countless ways and, quite honestly, they've probably been with us through the toughest, darkest times in our lives loving us unconditionally, beaming their love onto us until we were able to see the light in our lives again. Of course we're going to have a hole in our hearts and cry! How can we not?

Now, truthfully, I never saw myself as a writer or an author. Quite frankly, I hate writing—that's the bottom line. I find it very difficult to do. The words never flowed easily, and still don't. Never in a million years did I ever think I would ever write a book, let alone a book on animal communication and the messages animals want humans to know. I collected anecdotes along the way, miracles so to speak, due to the constant encouragement of my mum, Irene; husband, Drummond; sister, Ainsley; dad, Lorne; bonus-mum, Rona; and my dear friend Laura. I think I did it more to appease them and get them off my back more than anything else.

This book has been in the making for the last five years, and I've fought it off every step of the way. I had no idea how

I was going to write this! I had no idea how I was going to pull this story out of the depths of my mind. What I neglected to remember was the fact that the animals were going to be writing through me, and all I needed to do was have a conversation with them and type what they were saying. (It's a good thing I type 85 wpm because they speed talk!)

Even though I believe I have zero writing skills and initially lacked any desire to write this book, my soul kept urging me with more and more internal pressure to get this book written and get it out to the masses. There was a sense of urgency to just get it done.

I have an inkling the animals were conspiring with my soul to get this book written and published. My soul kept nagging me at the back of my mind to just put fingers to keyboard and start writing. I believe that a part of writing this book now is also due to the onslaught of animals who transition every year between October to December, which I call the Death Months. I can bet on it. It's with 100% certainty that I will always have more clients, then, who must make the hard decision to let their animals go versus clients who need energy work or a communication session in general.

As clinically trained as I am to create and hold the space needed for people to take their time to say goodbye to their beloved animal companions, it always weighs heavily on my heart.

Part of the urgency of writing this book has been due to experiencing people's pain on a regular basis when someone is deciding to euthanize their beloved animal companion. The number one question is always, "Is it time to let them go?" The number two question is generally, "Am I making the right decision?" Since I'm an empath, I feel people's pain and, really, all I want to be able to do is to relieve people and help them ease their hearts and minds of suffering and grief. The animals have called upon me to channel their thoughts, their wisdom, and their experience of how they navigate the dying and death journey.

This book's aim is to ease your mind and heart with a greater understanding and knowledge of their death and dying experiences and process and what happens when they transition from the physical into spirit. The way I explain it and remind my clients is the first law of thermodynamics, that energy can't be created or destroyed, it can only change from one form to another. For example, the chemical makeup of water is H_2O whether it's in a liquid, frozen, gas, or vapor form, but it's still water in essence. That's the same for our animals' essence, energy, soul—it changes from physical to ethereal.

This book is to pique people's interest and open their minds to other possibilities about animals' experiences with death and dying. This book is for anyone who has just the slightest curiosity or interest in how animal communication works and getting to know their animals better. It may also be of interest to people who already have a working knowledge of how telepathy works. Whether you're new to this topic or already somewhat aware, you'll come to learn how thoughts are transmitted using intention and vibration and the myriad wisdom animals have shared with me through telepathy.

This book is for those who are desperate to understand what is happening to their animal while they're ill or going through the death and dying process. For those who are trying to ease their grieving hearts. Or for those in a moment in time when they need and want to make the best decision for their animal. It's for those who are open to developing their understanding of transitioning from this physical reality to the spiritual realm and that life exists after we all "leave our raincoats" behind.

I can't promise you this book will have all the answers, but it will help you one way or another to gain a broader and deeper connection to your animals and a greater understanding of their death and dying experiences. My genuine hope for you is three-fold.

One, to gain insight on your animals' needs, wants, preferences and desires. To be able to see your animals, not as pets, but as companions, as sentient beings, who are compassionate, who serve us, and who are equal to us and not as a pet to own.

Two, that because of reading this book you'll have a deeper connection with and gratitude for your animals' presence in your lives and a better understanding of your animals.

Three, that you receive relief from the pain and suffering of losing a loved one and a peace of mind regarding your animals' journey in death.

Turn the page when you're ready and we will begin…

PART 1

A Primer on Animal Communication, Channeling, and Consciousness

CHAPTER I

DEFINING ANIMAL COMMUNICATION, CONSCIOUSNESS, AND CHANNELLING

It's not uncommon for a person's first interaction with an animal communicator (or telepath) to be from a place of desperation rather than awareness. In other words, most first-time clients have never worked with an animal communicator, nor do they understand the communicator's role or how it all works. They reach out because they are at a loss, having tried every other avenue they can think of to resolve a challenge or issue with a beloved animal. I often hear things such as:

"We've tried everything and we're desperate."

"We don't know where else to turn."

"You were recommended to me by a relative, friend, or my veterinarian."

"The veterinarians have checked out my dog/cat/bird/ rabbit/horse etc., and there's nothing physically wrong with him/her."

"I can't get my cat to stop peeing/pooping outside the litter box."

"I can't get my dog to stop being aggressive to other dogs and my vet wants me to put him on Prozac/Gabapentin and I don't want to but yet I can't let my animal to continue to suffer like this."

In other words, I am typically the last resort and usually because my client doesn't feel they have clarity or resolution around what is ailing their animal or adding to their abnormal mood or behavior.

During these desperate times, even the biggest skeptic will seriously consider booking an animal communication session. These are people who normally don't believe in psychics; they usually see them as woo-woo, head in the sky people who are out of touch with reality. However, they love their animals so much they're willing to put their own beliefs aside and try anything, even if that includes talking with an animal telepath/ psychic/communicator. Most of the time these types of clients book an initial consult because they have so many questions.

Melodie was once a skeptic who had no familiarity or awareness of animal communication until she came across my booth at a local farmer's market. It wasn't so much the sign I had hung that encouraged her to speak with me, but that I was friendly and outgoing. Melodie was having issues with her cat, Poncho, who was peeing in the kitchen sink and on the furniture. When she ventured my way, she told herself she needed to keep an open mind and not have any expectations—that it was okay to just be curious.

Melodie was open enough to allow me to channel her animal and, as a result, she learned the issue was with how Melodie perceived Poncho as just another object around the house. Additionally, Poncho was trying to communicate that she disliked the litter in her box. I gave Melodie some practical suggestions to help with the peeing problem, but also spoke with Melodie about the sentient nature of animals. Both things had a huge impact in how Melodie saw animals, but also how she began to interact with Poncho. (You'll hear more of Melodie and Poncho's story in Chapter 3–specifically from Poncho's perspective.)

Melodie was totally new to animal communication but, by being open to the possibility of animal telepathy and curious enough to allow for me to communicate with Poncho, a whole new world opened to her that had transformative results for her, Poncho, and their household.

You might have selected this book for reasons like Melodie or my other first-time clients' experiences. The purpose of this chapter is to offer you answers to the most frequently asked questions of my new clients. I think it's worth spending a chapter (or two) laying some foundation before we dive into the deeper content of this book. It might be hard to grapple with what I'm telling you about animal communication, consciousness, and channelling if I don't first define what these words mean and explain how each appears in the work I do. So, consider this chapter your 101 course.

What is communication?

Humans communicate in many ways with each other through words, body language, facial expressions, and tone of voice. Behind every subtle gesture lies meaning and energy directed to the other person. For example, we can sense when something isn't right or well with another or when a place, person, or thing isn't safe. There is energy exchanged between people—love, anger, fear. Our human eyes may not be able to see energy, but our bodies feel it. This transmission then gives information about the person or situation. When we think of communication in this way—as energy—rather than assuming it's all about spoken and written words, it's not hard to see how one can communicate with non-speaking beings like animals.

What is animal communication?

Animal communication describes the art of finding a nonverbal language through which we can understand animals, usually our animal companions. Animal communicators, telepaths, and psychics work to bridge our worlds, helping us determine what the animals in our lives need or are trying to tell us. There are subtle differences between animal communicators or telepaths and psychics even though the general public might think they are all the same. From my perspective, the words "animal communicator" and "telepath" can be used interchangeably and are similar in practice as they are both about tapping into the energy field and then using the heart vibration frequency to communicate with the animal.

An animal "psychic", in my opinion, is a bit different in that they sense the animal's energy field (on the surface) without going deeper into their vibration but can still predict or assume what's happening with the animal with some level of accuracy. For the purposes of this book, I'll be using the words "animal communicator" and "telepath" and speaking from those places as that is the lens from which I can speak. As animal communicators, it's up to us to practice getting out of our heads and thoughts and into our hearts, focusing on empathy and feelings or emotions.

People who work in this field say communicating works using telepathy or "distance feeling"—communication through distance (tele) and with emotions/energies (pathy) from empathy, which is the ability to see what is in someone else's mind, to feel their feelings, or to communicate with them without using words or other physical signals. A perfect example of telepathic communication is when we're thinking of someone and that person calls a few minutes later. It's when a mother knows when something has happened to her child or fur kid.

Before there was the ability to write and read, we were all able to communicate through telepathic communication. It was through reading and writing that programmed us to believe the only way to communicate is through the spoken/written word. Over time, the ability to telepathically communicate diminished to the point where people believed (and still do) that it's not possible to telepathically communicate or only those who are "gifted" can do it.

So, when it comes to being an animal telepath, we must deprogram the belief that we can't telepathically communicate. How do you think animals communicate with each other? We must unlearn our cultural programming to depend on thinking and begin to really trust our instincts about information we're receiving from the animal. The message is usually the first thing that comes to mind, yet it's the first thing we tend to discount because it happens so fast.

What is the difference between animal communication, channeling, and consciousness?

Animal communication is about having a conversation with an animal. I ask them a question and they give me an answer. Animal channeling, from my perspective and lived experience, is *embodying* the animal. It's not just hearing them, but also feeling them in my body. It's receiving all their messages and presence in any form in which they arrive.

Animals communicate in words, pictures, movies, sentences, physical, and emotional sensations to each other and to us. When communicating, I can receive these stimuli (words, pictures, movies, sentences) in conversation with the animal without embodying them (such as receiving physical and emotional sensations). It can be a casual conversation the same way one might have coffee with a friend and talk about what's new in their world.

Other times, when I need to dig deeper into what they're communicating, I channel them. I embody them in a way that enables me to see what they see. I hear what they hear, and I feel what they feel. I'm able to project my mind into the animals' bodies, hence, I essentially become them. I can then feel the pain they may have or taste the food they dislike.

For example, I was contacted by a woman who had a serious riding accident with her horse, Walter, to the point that it not only severely shook them both up, but they were both injured, her right leg and ankle and his right knee, shoulder and wrist. It took them both several weeks to physically heal. She said they couldn't return to their ease with one another after, and lessons became a chore rather than an enjoyment as they used to be. After being introduced to Walter, I projected my mind into his body and immediately he took me through the accident from his perspective. My upper body started to curl forward and my right hand at the wrist started to curl under. I sensed into the bottom of Walter's hoof, a.k.a. my hand, and there was a large stone that he tripped and buckled over. My whole body then started going forward and to the right demonstrating to his human how he collapsed on her right leg and ankle. He explained to me that he failed in his job to keep his human safe and felt awful about it. He said that he did his best to keep her on his back but once his shoulder gave in, his rider's leg and ankle were caught under him. He said he felt so guilty and was ashamed of himself and didn't know how to make it up to her.

Once my client heard Walter's explanation, she immediately told him that she felt guilty for not being more observant of how rocky the ground was and that she felt so responsible for his injuries, and she felt awful about it. Also, those combined feelings were causing the block between them. It was an incredible deep-hearted connection and conversation about how they both took personal responsibility for one other's injuries. They both said there was nothing to forgive because they loved each other so deeply and accidents did happen, and they would always be together. About two months later, I got a wonderful report from my client saying they'd been having joyful rides and lessons together and it seemed to her they were back to their ease and enjoyment of each other's company.

Animal consciousness is different than both communication and channeling as this is not an action or activity that I perform with the animal. Consciousness is a state of being aware. Just as humans have consciousness—self-awareness of their physical, intellectual, and emotional self—so do animals. Animals have the same awareness but different ways of expressing this awareness. All beings have consciousness, and what's important is understanding this so we don't objectify our animals and therefore treat them as inferior, lesser beings.

When we think about how animal communication, channeling and consciousness work together; I know that animals have consciousness by what they can communicate to me through their energy fields while we are having a conversation or by what I experience when I embody them through channelling.

Who do animals communicate with?

Animals communicate with each other and with humans. Their thoughts are just as real as ours; they transmit and receive information through words, emotions, physical sensations and images. It doesn't matter if I'm working on a dog who's only heard German all her life, it's the Universal Oneness (Source, God, Spirit, The Divine) that becomes the translator for both of us.

Animals communicate with each other on the physical, mental, emotional, and spiritual levels all at once to determine who is who, who is part of their pack/pride, who is head of their group, who is their enemy, and who is safe or not. One horse, Hemi, shared that they talk with each other through their voices (i.e. their neighs) and connect their minds and hearts and pass information on to each other. They don't have to be face to face as a whole herd. They are still able to transfer information and knowledge when they're separated, and that's because of animals' oversoul and their ability to speak to one another.

One of my closest horse friends, Trick, once described the oversoul as being of one mind:

> *"It's a group mind, like bees and ants. There is one soul directing all the hundreds and trillions of bees and ants. They experience the knowingness of connection and beingness of the One Mind. The oneness of it all. It's like the murmuration of starlings.*
>
> *"When you look up in the sky and you see the beautiful dance patterns of the starlings, humans ask 'how do they know how to do this?' Well, that's the oversoul—the hive-mind directing them and communicating to each other all at once at the same time in the same moment. As horses, we have a hive mind, but we are also separate.*
>
> *"We are sentient beings; we talk with each other telepathically. However, we have our own minds, too, and our own thoughts, experiences, traumas, loves. We feel, sense, and are individuals, but we communicate all together at once which is how you can see a herd running through the field together and then suddenly, we'll stop and immediately turn around to run the other way if we feel we're in danger. That's just one example of how we collectively think and communicate in this way."*

What do animals communicate about?

Animals communicate with humans and other animals about their thoughts, feelings, preferences, joy, annoyance, sorrow, physical discomfort. For all the things humans communicate about, animals do, too. Hemi shared:

> *"We talk about our day, who came to ride us, what it was like, which humans are kind, which humans have frustration and anger in their hearts and to stay away from those if possible. We talk about daily activities in the barn, our experiences, and we tell one another what happened during our rides and what happened with our riders. Sometimes we roll our eyes at our riders, other times we're laughing at them and sometimes we're angry and frustrated because they weren't listening to us. Sometimes we're full of joy because we had fun more times than not.*
>
> *Just know that we're watching and listening to everything you say, and we take it all in. We know and understand more than you think we do, more than you give us credit for."*

Nacho, a friend of a friend's dog, described animals communicating to one another as "gab fests" when animals play with each other. Specifically, he said:

> *"We're transferring information to one another. We have our complaints. I flash pictures and images to the other dogs I'm playing with about what I'm upset about, and then we play it out and it's out of my system. We do the same for one another. Playing, play-fighting, chasing each other—it's a lot of fun and so necessary for us because it's a stress reliever and it's really needed."*

Why would someone call in an animal communicator? What are the benefits?

There are myriad reasons someone might call an animal communicator, but here is the shortlist:

- Strengthening the human and their animal companion's bond.

- Reducing stress and anxiety for both the human and their animal friend.

- Understanding each other's needs.

- Bringing in a new animal—when humans want to introduce a new animal to the home, they need to check in with the other animal residents how they feel about having a new fur-friend join the group.

- Communicating about vacations—when the humans are leaving, for how long, where they are going, who will be taking care of them.

- Preparing the animals for life transitions such as: moving, new baby, renovations of a home, divorce/separation.

- Explaining why they're going to the vet's and what they can expect.

- Determining what's wrong with an animal—When veterinarians have determined there is nothing physically wrong with an animal patient, they will refer these patients to an animal communicator to hear from the animal what may be going on that's negatively impacting their mental or emotional wellness.

- Understanding behavioral changes and challenges—when our fur kids' behavior becomes distressing to both humans and animals in the home such as separation anxiety, aggression, urinating or pooping outside of the litter box, plucking feathers, refusing to move out from under the bed, or obsessive grooming.

- Making the decision to euthanize and let them go— when the time comes that the animal is close to passing away, their humans will contact me to make a joint decision with their animal as to how much longer the animal wants to stay in their body, if they want to pass away on their own volition, or if they feel they need help from a veterinarian.

Now, I do want to mention here that sometimes people will contact me to help them find a lost animal. I usually turn them down because this is not my area of expertise. I specialize as a wellness intuitive, and I always make it clear with clients they need to take their animals to their veterinarian's office if they're at all concerned about the animals' health. However, what I can do is let them know if their animal is still alive or not, and that's because I sense and feel into whether that extra individual energy (frequency of the physical body) is present or not, and I ask them if they're in their body or have left it just to validate what I've sensed.

What's the difference between communicating with living animals versus the spirits/souls of those who have passed?

There are very slight differences for me when I'm talking with animals who are still living in their physical bodies versus those who have transitioned out of their bodies. When I'm talking with an animal who is still in the physical, there's a life energy force around their body that I tap into. It's a vibration or what I call their individualistic energy signature that I sense. There's not a single animal I've spoken with who has the same frequency—no two energy signatures or frequencies are the same. It's the same for humans; there are no two fingerprints that are the same in the world—they're unique to that individual.

For those animals who have passed on, their energies are "lighter", not as dense as previously when in their body; there's a "flatness" I sense in them that's there when they've died. In the bodies there's a wholeness, a three-dimensional feel to them, whereas when they're out of body, it's very light, more two-dimensional.

The soul has its own frequency, but when it's put into a physical body, that body has its own energy signature and frequency that seems to overlap and override the soul's energy. When the body dies, that body's energy frequency also dies and the Soul's energy frequency remains, hence the lighter sense.

When I communicate with animals' souls, there's a deeper wisdom that comes forward–more insightful, wiser, more philosophical than previously when they were in their bodies. If I've worked with an animal prior to its dying, the personality of the animal is present; it experiences fear, nervousness, anxiety, pain, and sadness that doesn't exist when the animal's soul leaves its body. Once it's left its body, the soul's wisdom of the animal is front and center. Its essence is pure love; it vibrates as love. The fear, sadness, anxiety, and pain are all gone. I've never sensed any of these expressions from the animals who have died.

Do you have to be physically present to communicate or channel an animal?

I do not have to be in the physical presence with an animal; I can easily do it over Zoom. My clients are from across the globe in Australia, Sweden, Germany, England, and throughout North America. Energy exists all at once and everywhere. Thoughts are transmitted through energy frequencies, and it follows intention which is how I'm able to telepathically communicate with animals no matter where they live.

Can anyone connect with their animals?

I would say yes, and my cat, Curious, agrees. Here's what she had to say about it (and keep in mind we'll be diving into some of these concepts in the next chapter):

> *"In order to connect with animals, you must start from a loving place. It's all about the heart and love. It's also about respect and what you're able to give to the animals in the moment of connection. For those of us living in humans' homes, we can't independently take care of ourselves; we need your help and cooperation. This is a partnership, and we need to be treated like a partner rather than an object. We are sentient beings. We have feelings, emotions…we understand everything that is going on in the home, with our humans and with other animals. It's hard to communicate when you're not connected to your hearts and you're always in your thoughts and mind.*
>
> *Spend some time sitting, meditating, connecting to the Universal love and reaching out with your mind's eye*

to other beings in this world, not just to humans. The objective is for us to work together as equals, to understand that we are partners on this planet, and we serve each other. We make you happy, do we not? We make you smile. You feel like children again when you play with us. It's that connection that helps you to remember who you truly are. You are a true essence of the Divine, of Universal Spirit that is in an ever-constant state of joy, love, and peace.

When you're with your animal, are you not in a state of peace even if it's for a few minutes? Pay attention to these times, remember how it feels to be in a state of peace, love and joy and let those feelings expand through your awareness into your everyday life. This is how animals serve our humans. Humans give their animals a place of peace, safety, joy; you help us grow, expand, and evolve. We learn more about human nature living with you. We need these experiences with humans to have a better understanding of what a human being is to be prepared for our own eventuality of becoming human."

How does it help if people listen to animals' wants and preferences?

Nacho's answer makes it perfectly clear what the benefits are of people listening to their animals:

"It tells me/us that the human respects me as a sentient being and that the person can be trusted. When we're overridden, it tells me that you don't care about what my wants/needs/ preferences are, but you care more

about yourself and what you're wanting in the moment without any regard for others."

I believe the most important thing to understand and lean into is the idea that you *can* communicate with your beloved animals. By working with an animal communicator (or telepath), you can learn directly from your animal(s) about their needs, desires, and preferences, and to develop a deeper understanding of who they are as sentient beings (more coming in Chapter 3). It's also possible for you to develop your own ability to communicate with your animals even if not to the same level of expertise as myself or another communicator. And that's what the next chapter is about—understanding and listening to your animals.

CHAPTER 2

UNDERSTANDING AND LISTENING TO OUR ANIMALS

Even though our animals were not born with the ability to form words, it doesn't mean they don't communicate with us. Animals communicate with us in many ways through shared physical sensations, emotions, and if paying attention, through their eyes. They are intelligent and sentient beings.

"Sentient" means capable of sensing and feeling, or conscious (as we discussed in the prior chapter). They understand what we say, and they can read our emotions. As Celeste, a horse, says, "We may be quiet, but we hear, see and feel everything...we know what is happening all around us. You may think we don't know what's being said but we can feel the energies of your intentions. Be mindful of what you say and how you talk to us. We understand more than you think we do."

The best comparison I can make is the way we can sense tension when walking into a room full of people and immediately know that something just happened or was said to cause tension in the group. How do we know that without someone telling us or explaining the situation? It's our energy fields; they hold our emotions, thoughts, intentions.

Carol Komitor, Founder of Healing Touch for Animals, defines the energy field as

> "...an electromagnetic field that surrounds and supports the body. Everything that leaves or comes into the body, including words, actions and intentions, passes through the energy field. The energy field collects the data of our life experiences and stores it."

In other words, each person's energy fields are sending and receiving information to one another. In a more animal-related example, how do our cats and dogs know when we're taking them to the veterinarian's and it's hard to get them into the carrier or the car, but we haven't said anything to them? They can read our intentions in our energy fields. Or how is it that our animals know when we're coming home and they're at the door waiting for us? It's because they can feel our energy field—our intentions of coming home—from a distance.

Activating your energy field

Energy doesn't understand time and distance—these are human-made constructs. Energy exists all at once, everywhere. Understanding energy is important to learning how to communicate with animals.

Start by rubbing your hands together to create friction and heat between your hands. Keep rubbing them until your hands are warm and vibrating. Now, hold your hands about an inch apart, keep your fingers together. This is where you really need to concentrate and zero your attention. Feel the pulsing of the energy you just activated between your hands.

As you feel the energy between your hands, create the shape of a ball as if you're holding a baseball in both hands. Feel the pulsing between your hands. If you can't feel the pulsing anymore, activate the energy again by rubbing your hands. Once you feel the shape of a baseball in your hands, expand your hands while still concentrating on the pulsating energy, and widen your hands into a beach ball. Now, focus your attention on the pulsating energy into the size of a beach ball and move your hands around the beach ball, feeling into it. You can play around with this by imagining you're seeing different colors and different shapes and sizes. Sometimes, keeping your eyes closed makes this exercise easier to sense. By doing this, you're also beginning to activate your third eye.

The third eye is your psychic vision or intuition center. It utilizes your pineal gland for increased spiritual awakening. It's located in the middle of your forehead just above the eyebrows, otherwise known as your sixth (or brow) chakra. Okay—what does this have to do with animal communication? It's about activating the energy field within you and around your body. It's also about helping you to sense what energy feels like, whether it's our own energy or someone else's. Even though most people can't see energy, we can at least activate it and start practicing what it feels like.

To me, energy looks like thermals coming from a hot sidewalk or tarmac, but it's located around people and animals at different frequencies and vibrations, otherwise known as the aura. The energy field of animals is ten times the size of that of humans, whereas human energy fields extend from the body out approximately eighteen inches. All of this is important to animal communication because it's all a part of it. I've mentioned before that I feel, see, and hear everything the animals feel, see, and hear, and this is because I'm attuned to their energy fields to the point that I essentially become them.

The next step is to reactivate your energy field by rubbing your hands together and, this time, imagine feeling the weight of your animal's paws in the palm of your hand. It doesn't matter which hand you choose. You already know how heavy or light your animal's paw is by the numerous times you've asked your dog to "shake a paw" or trying, sometimes with very little success, to trim your cat's nails. Just imagine feeling that weight in your hand; sense your animal's paw in your hand. If you have an aquatic animal, imagine them swimming above the palm of your hand. Put intention towards this exercise because energy follows intention. You'll eventually feel a fish swimming around just slightly above your hand. The same can be said for any animal. However, if you have a horse, what I would suggest is that you feel what it's like holding your horse's hoof as if you're just about to clean it. Imagine that you can feel that weight of the hoof, feel the heat coming off the leg of the horse against your body. Imagination plays a significant role in activating the energy field and works in tandem with intention and intuition.

Imagination, intention, intuition, and reading energy

When you use your imagination, you have to use your intention, and energy follows intention. This is just the beginning of how to feel energy which you can then use to start communicating with your animal. It's necessary to understand what energy is and what it feels like so you know how to read energy and communicate with it.

Once you've experienced what energy feels like and you've practiced a bit, you must trust your intuition. Intuition is energy; it's a sense of knowing. Intuition is also called clairsentience which means, clear feeling. Britannica defines intuition as "a natural ability or power that makes it possible to know something without any proof or evidence: a feeling that guides a person to act a certain way without fully understanding why."

Animal communication is mainly about feeling, sensing, and using intuition to interpret what your animal is telling you. Not trusting one's intuition is the biggest block people have when it comes to animal communication. Over time as you consistently practice, you'll trust your intuition more and begin to know that you're truly hearing what your animal is telling you.

Getting started with animal communication

As long as you're able to put your ego aside—including your doubts and negative thinking—as long as you can trust your instincts and believe in yourself, you can take the plunge into the incredible, eye-opening world of animal communication. It's about getting out of your own way.

So, to begin, reflect on these questions:

- Are your intentions to communicate honorable, pure, clean, true, honest and for a higher good?

- Do you trust your instincts?

- Do you believe in yourself to even try?

- Are you able to put your ego aside and use your heart instead?

- Can you remember that you are an animal, too, of the human species?

Then, to practice communicating with your fur-friend, ask a family member or a friend who has an animal of their own to send you a front-facing picture of their animal, and write down five questions that only your family member/friend would know the answers to. Make sure you ask them to make the questions easy, such as questions with one-word answers to start.

I always find looking at the eyes and sensing into them is a great way to connect with an animal's energy field. Once you get a sense of that animal, close your eyes, move your mind's eye to your heart, and ask one of the questions. Write down the very first split-second answer that comes to mind. You'll instinctively want to doubt yourself, but don't. Most of the time, the very first thing that comes to mind is the answer. When you start to doubt yourself, the answer vanishes and something more logical will come to mind.

For instance, when I was re-learning my communication abilities, I was practicing with a friend of mine who also was learning the method with me at the same time. She asked my cat, Tenderfoot, what her favorite food was, and my girlfriend immediately came up with scrambled eggs. My friend immediately doubted herself and told me that the answer didn't make sense to her, but she said that scrambled eggs are what immediately came to her mind. I confirmed that, in fact, scrambled eggs were (and still are) Tenderfoot's favorite meal. My girlfriend said she was going to override that answer and say salmon instead but then refused to give into the doubt. Needless to say, she was surprised and relieved to know that scrambled eggs were the right answer, and the confidence she had about her abilities became stronger. Continue this practice until you believe that you can ask your animal simple questions you've always wondered about them and receive accurate answers.

Animal behaviour is communication

Your animal is communicating with you all the time, whether it be by staring at you or using their voice to get your attention (by chirping, squawking, barking, or meowing). They're communicating to you through behavioral language by not eating or by peeing or pooping outside the litter box, displaying separation anxiety, destroying furniture, scratching, biting, chewing, hissing, purring, wagging their tails, softening their eyes, or dropping their heads when you're petting them or talking to them sweetly.

Barking or making noise is also a way animals are attempting to communicate. As one dog, Blackjack, puts it:

> *"We have to protect our premises. I don't understand why humans tell dogs to be quiet when we bark when someone enters our house perimeter. We're on guard, that's our job. We're sort of like an alarm system."*

But that isn't the only reason a dog may use their voice to try to get their human's attention. Sometimes, they want you to play with them, take them for a walk, or to go off leash.

Animals' behavior IS their way of communicating to you. We, as their human companions, have to become aware of their behaviors and what they're trying to tell us, such as the very simple example of when dogs or cats sit in front of doors to indicate they want to be let out, or when your animals run to the door when you come home; it always feels so great to me when my cats come running to the door to greet me!

When you find your cat or dog hiding in the closet or under the bed, ask yourself what's going on in your life or in the home that would contribute to them hiding? Is the homelife so busy it's whirling around them like a tornado? Are there a lot of people and strangers coming in and out of the home? Are there any other animals in the home acting the same way? Are the animals interacting well with one another, or are there hostile interactions happening between them? Any disruption in daily routines may cause your animal to display unwanted behavior. We need to figure out what's happening in their world that would cause them to behave in a way that's concerning, or on the other hand, enjoy the moments when they're playful, purring, or wanting attention.

Here's how Nacho would explain animal communication:

> *"We sure can talk with humans, but it's whether or not they want to hear what we have to say. Sure, we use our voices when we bark and employ our body movements and behaviors, but it's up to them to really understand what we're telling them. Just because we don't have the ability to form words doesn't mean we don't understand what they're telling us.*
>
> *I can read and tell by their energy fields, their intentions, their thoughts, and how their energies are when they get up in the mornings whether they're in a good mood or a bad mood. I know that if they're in a good mood, I can get away with certain things I normally wouldn't be allowed to do."*

When I asked for an example, Nacho replied:

"You know every day little things such as their ignoring me when I'm sniffing in the garbage 'cause they know that I really don't want to get into it. I just want to smell what is in it. I don't necessarily want to eat it. If they're in a bad mood, I know well enough to stay away from the garbage; I don't need them to start yelling at me to get away from it. If they're in a good mood, I can get away with certain things I normally wouldn't be allowed to do, like sniffing the trash."

By sensing and using your animal's communication behaviours, we can figure out a lot about what's going on with them and then attend to their specific needs or wants. Sometimes, it's just a matter of changing one's perception of an animal that is owned versus seeing them as sentient beings that are equal to us. They may have a different way of communicating than we do, but they *are* communicating. It's just a bit harder to understand them when they're not able to speak directly with us. We as humans must be aware and present to notice how our animals are communicating with us. We all can talk to or communicate with animals. It's only a matter of believing we can do it.

CHAPTER 3

THEY'RE NOT PETS, THEY'RE SENTIENT BEINGS

Over the years of communicating with all types of animals, one of the main messages they want humans to understand is they are sentient beings and not just objects to have as pets. They have human companions, not owners. They desperately want us to learn that animals are compassionate, intelligent; they sense, see, and know things that the human body just doesn't have the ability to experience. This is due to our social conditioning which directs humans to feel unworthy, fearful, and undervalued.

Let's return to Melodie and Poncho for a moment. Melodie was at a point of desperation because her cat Poncho kept peeing on the furniture and in the kitchen sink. When Melodie allowed me to channel Poncho, Poncho was able to communicate that part of the issue was she didn't like the litter material in her litter box and the other issue had to do with the fact that she didn't like being viewed as another object in the house. I was able to communicate this (and more) to Melodie and things completely shifted. When I asked Poncho later to describe the change, this was what Poncho shared:

> *"Going from being seen as a pet to an equal is night and day. My human didn't understand that I was an equal. She saw me as an object and that my brother and I were owned by the family. She really didn't have much to do with me or my brother. She saw us as one more thing to be taken care of versus having a deep, connected relationship like we have now. Once the lightbulb went off in her head, everything between us changed.*
>
> *She was listening to what I had to say through my behaviors. She took me into consideration when making changes and because I could feel that energy switch, I started to act and behave in a way that showed her I understood her, that I knew she was changing her perspective on us and seeing us in an entirely different way.*
>
> *For instance, when she just saw me as a pet that was just another object to be taken care of, I used to pee in the sink because I didn't like my litter. She just saw my behavior as a nuisance; meanwhile, I was trying to communicate to her that I wasn't unhappy with the litter in my box. I didn't want litter in my box; I didn't want anything in my box—I wanted an empty box where I could pee. I thought peeing in a sink would be quite practical, since there's running water, and it would go down the drain.*
>
> *So, when I finally got a chance to speak to Melodie through Karen, I was able to ask why she had us when it was very clear that she didn't want us around and*

didn't spend much time with us. That was the lightbulb moment for Melodie. She saw how our behaviors were trying to tell her that something was wrong. We wanted her help and her attention, and we wanted her to want us.

Melodie did a complete 180 and saw us as equals. She immediately switched out the litter from the box, tilted the box so my urine would puddle in a corner and my paws wouldn't get wet and I stopped peeing in the sinks. She also spent more time with us and our relationship has become mutually loving and deeper."

Now, Melodie wasn't intentionally treating the animals like objects. Most of us who don't consider ourselves animal people or pet lovers aren't attempting to purposefully demean our animal companions. We lack the understanding, awareness, education, or cultural expectation that animals are to be treated as equals. It's not mainstream to believe that animals have consciousness in the same way humans do.

In the case of Melodie and Poncho, Melodie wasn't aware that Poncho could feel the resentment she had about Poncho's behavior or that it was making Poncho's behavior worse. We all carry internal baggage that can impact our animals. Our animals feel it all—from our energy to our attitude in the morning, to things that make us angry. We must see our animals as a part of the family, just like our children are.

An animal's purpose

Animals want us to know they choose who they will be spending their lives with, helping their humans through comfort, love, patience, compassion, empathy, and above all—love.

They serve humanity in these ways as their higher purpose. They help us navigate the difficult emotions in life. They are loyal to us; they love us unconditionally and they are our greatest teachers. They want us to know they hear and understand their humans; it's the humans who have difficulty hearing and understanding them. The bottom line is that animals are not objects to be owned or mastered.

My cat, Tenderfoot puts it like this:

> *"We're not objects you can just pickup and hold at your own will, whenever you want to. We're not push-button toys that will do as you say. We're beings who have our own thoughts, our own desires, and our own preferences. We're not owned; we're individual beings who have chosen to be a part of your life. We're not something you just picked out of a litter or bought from a breeder or chose at a rescue facility. We're living, breathing creatures who walk this earth just as humans do. We have the same basic needs just as humans do—food, water, and safe shelter. To me, the word 'pet' has a connotation that I'm to be owned, mastered, or lorded over, being dictated without any say, without being taken into consideration.*

> *"There are instances when I depend upon my humans to make the right decisions for me regarding my health. My body language will tell my humans when something is wrong. For instance, when I had hyperthyroidism, my human knew that something was severely wrong because my behaviors and health drastically changed within a two-week timeframe. This was an obvious,*

exaggerated example; I depended on my humans to figure out what was wrong with me and to make medical decisions that I couldn't.

However, it was done with respect. I was cared for as an equal, the right things took place medically, and I was fine in the long run. There are exceptions to what I'm saying because I'm not able to take care of myself in that kind of way. If a human sees their animal as a pet, that changes the dynamic of the relationship altogether; they don't have as connected a relationship. It's more a hierarchy of superior (human) to inferior (animal) behavior versus an equal relationship. This dynamic isn't great, but it's not bad either; it's just a disconnected relationship that animals may experience with their humans.

"We know they love us, we know they care deeply for us and would do anything for us, but what's missing is the deep heart-sense that goes along with treating your animals as if they are equal to you versus a better-than-you relationship."

Hemi agrees with their sentiments. *"Nobody owns anything. Owning an animal is a human construct. We are all sentient beings. We love, we communicate in a non-human way, we feel, we're emotional creatures. I am not any more valuable than the bird who is singing a song about her day, telling her bird friends."*

My cat, Curious, would summarize everything from this chapter to these ideas:

"Animals aren't pets. We're living, highly intelligent beings. We're not objects to be owned. We're animals

who have feelings, who are emotional, who have likes and dislikes. We're not just another pretty, live doll. Treat us as if we're another human being! Be respectful, listen to our voices, and to how we convey messages to you through our voices and body language. Know that we are equal to you. Don't just assume that we have a behavioral problem when we do something you consider as "bad." Take that opportunity to question why we do that? Ask yourself if you set up the environment for your animals' best interest. A lot of our behavior is a direct reflection of how humans in our lives treat us. A lot of the time, animal behavior is a mirror that's reflecting things back to our humans, but they don't want to look at their own ways of interacting with us or with one another and would rather just chalk it up to the cat being bad."

PART 2

Animal Wisdom and
Messages About Living

CHAPTER 4

ON THE IMPORTANCE OF FOOD

Food is such a broad topic, yet I find it so necessary because many issues people bring to me are about food and allergies. Again, I'm not a veterinarian, and animals' diets and nutrition should always be discussed first with your veterinarian. I'm strictly writing from the animals' perspective, preferences, patterns and trends based on what I've repeatedly heard over the last ten-plus years in my professional animal communication practice. The information provided in this chapter is what I commonly hear from animals about their food on a regular basis.

Here's Tenderfoot's perspective on the importance of food:

"If I can talk about anything it'd be about food! Food is so incredibly important, from the type and taste to the texture of food. People should know that regular feeding times are important. Predictability is important at least for me because it tells me that I don't have to worry about food and when it's coming. I get nervous when I'm not fed at my usual time. I know my parents

have never missed a meal, but I can't help it, I just get nervous. If you can't feed your animals on time, please just tell them and they'll understand. That way, they won't be so nervous and wondering if they'll be fed at all. Just say it out loud to them; they'll understand and will relax. Just tell them what the new time is instead of making them wonder and worry. You must understand, we're dependent on you, our humans, to feed us. We don't have food otherwise; we can't go out to hunt to fend for ourselves. So, just please give us the courtesy of a time when you'll feed us if you can't be on time."

Offering a variety

One of the main things I commonly hear from animals is that their food is boring; it's the same thing for breakfast, lunch, and dinner so there's no variety. Some animals don't like how dry their dry food is, but they'll tolerate it when water is added. When I project myself into their bodies and I focus on the dry food coming into their mouths, my own mouth immediately becomes bone dry, and my body feels dehydrated because so much of their body's moisture is used to break down and digest their food. Tenderfoot explains it this way:

"People think they can feed us the same type of food over and over again—the same flavor and the same type—and it'll be okay for us. WRONG!! Would you like to eat the same thing for breakfast, lunch, and dinner every day? Can you imagine eating cereal for every meal of your life? No! It becomes boring and it's hard on the stomach. We stop taking nutrition into our systems and we become hypersensitive to the same foods all the

time. I've had dry, wet, and raw foods of all types of meat. There was a time when my parents would only feed me canned turkey because that's the only protein my system could handle for a long while. It worked for the first six months or so but afterwards I started vomiting that up. They then started me on raw food and different types of meats—I mean meats I've never tasted before like kangaroo, salmon, elk, deer, camel, and wild boar. There are a ton of different flavors when they mix them up for each meal. My body loves this! I'm stronger, I have more energy, and my fur is lighter, not so dense and thick but fluffy as it should be. I rarely vomit now, and I can hardly wait until I get my next meal!"

When animals complain about having the same food every meal of every day, their comment to their human is usually "How would you like to have toast for breakfast, lunch and dinner day in and day out?" That's when my clients will usually understand that not having any variety in their animals' food can't be pleasant. I always suggest that my clients give a variety of protein and different tastes to keep food interesting. You'll see that your animal will be more eager to eat, happier, and enthusiastic when it comes to dinner time.

Prescription diets and food sensitivities

Now, there are some animals who come to me on prescription diets for one reason or another. We need to always check the ingredients of the food, prescription diets or not. I have many clients who say their animal won't stop scratching or won't stop licking their paws or stomach and there's no fur left or there's too much dandruff. When I project my mind into their bodies, I immediately feel either the itchiness, the irritation, or the inflammation on their skin. I then ask if they're ingesting chicken or pork, and nine times out of ten the answer is yes!

I always, always encourage my clients to talk with their veterinarian about the nutritional needs and dietary requirements for their animals. I also suggest they talk with their veterinarians about the possibility their animal may be allergic to chicken and/or pork. The feedback I receive from such clients a few months later is that they replaced chicken with turkey and took pork out of their animals' diets and their animals stopped the scratching or licking behaviors and the dandruff disappeared.

Raw food versus canned food

Honeybee, my sister, Ainsley's, semi-feral cat, spends most of her days outside if it's not raining. She recently had a few teeth removed due to decay, so I thought I would take the opportunity to talk with her about her recent experience of eating canned food versus raw food. After having her teeth removed, she wasn't allowed to eat her usual raw food for twelve days.

Me: What do you think of your raw food?

HB: I love raw food because of all the different flavors. It's delicious, it's moist, juicy, it's as if I killed my own prey to eat, but it's not warm. It's out of the cooling machine.

(She shows me the refrigerator.)

Me: You recently had a couple of teeth removed and you weren't allowed to eat raw food for twelve days. Can you please tell me what you ate instead?

HB: I ate canned food. I hated it. I absolutely hated it! I mean, there wasn't any taste, it was bland, it was dull, it was yucky. I had to go for days eating this yucky, bland food until my gums healed. I was hungry so of course I ate it, but it wasn't enjoyable. There's something that happens with the food when it goes from raw to canned, bland foods. Whatever it is, it takes the yummy out of it. It just tastes dead. I mean, I know the food is dead to begin with, but it isn't alive like the raw food. The raw food has blood in it, there's moisture, it's not changed, and the flavors are alive in my mouth; it's not bland at all.

After surgery on my mouth, not only did I not feel good for a couple of days but on top of it I had to eat this awful stuff that I didn't consider food. My skin felt dry and tight all over my body, and I couldn't get my skin to feel better. I felt sluggish. I didn't have the same kind of energy level I'm used to. There was a lack of pep in my step, if you know what I mean.

Me: Is this because you underwent surgery, and your body could be recuperating?

HB: Sure, for the first few days but not the whole time. I wasn't allowed to eat the "alive" food. I didn't bounce back until Mum gave me the raw food after my gums healed. Plus, my gums healed faster too once I got back onto the raw food, it was healing slowly on the bland food.

Do you think that humans actually taste the cat food they make for cats?

Me: I don't know for sure, but I'm quite confident the humans don't taste test the processed food.

HB: If they tasted it, they wouldn't serve it to animals.

I projected my mind into Honeybee's body to get a better understanding of how she felt when eating the processed food. I imagined putting raw food into my mouth and experiencing its juicy texture. My mouth started to water. It had different and interesting flavors; it made eating enjoyable and not just a chore. When I then imagined putting the canned, processed food into my mouth, I immediately understood what Honeybee meant by stating that it tasted dead and bland compared to raw food. I then imagined letting the processed food go through her body's systems to assess how her body reacted to the food. I instantly felt a slowing down of energy; my skin felt tight and dry, it was difficult to move around, I was not as flexible. It felt like all the moisture was zapped out of the canned food and, by extension, out of me.

I can certainly now understand Honeybee's perspective and why she doesn't really like the canned, processed/bland food. In my process of experiencing her consuming raw food, I felt her body's systems come back on, as though the switches were turned on all at once. Her body felt hydrated, flexible, plump, bendable, and the flavors of the raw food were so different.

When I asked Honeybee if there was anything else she wanted to say about canned versus raw food, she said:

"I don't know what humans are thinking about when they process food. It's not fun eating it. It's not natural and it doesn't taste good at all. I certainly hope I never have surgery again because I don't want to have to ever eat canned food again. I love my raw food."

Eating Live Prey—A Cat's Perspective

Britta was a beautiful old cat who transitioned at 18 years old. Before she transitioned, she explained to me that eating birds was not a big deal. Britta explained herself:

> *"I don't understand why people get so upset about it! It's our nature. Catching, hunting, preying. It's how we keep our minds sharp. We need to solve problems, hone our skills; it's just who we are. I ask that people don't get so upset when we bring home the prizes whether it's mice, birds, or other little creatures such as moles. It's who we are; it's part of the deal when you bring us into your home."*

I asked Britta how humans should react when it comes to their bringing a feathered or other "prize" home. She replied:

> *"Praise us with appreciation and admiration for our hunting skills. Understand just how much strategy, talent, and skill it takes to accomplish catching not only mice but especially birds."*

Now that you are attuned to the importance of food for animals, you can tune in to your animal's response to food. It may be that your animal is perfectly content with their diet. Or perhaps something in this chapter has you considering whether a change may be necessary. If that's the case, remember that this chapter does not replace the professional guidance from your veterinarian. You should make an appointment to discuss with them your questions and concerns. And, of course, you can also call upon an animal communicator to speak with your animal to verify their food preferences and desires.

CHAPTER 5

SAFETY, PERMISSION,
AND BOUNDARIES

Having animals in our lives requires that we take safety—ours, theirs and others—into account. We must make clear boundaries for them, but we also need to take into consideration their boundaries and preferences. This chapter focuses on these aspects from the animals' perspective, experience, and point of view.

Cats' safety: indoors or outdoors?

When people think of safety for their cats, one of the more difficult decisions to make is whether they'll be indoor cats, fully outdoor cats, and/or a combination of indoor/outdoor cats. People want to make sure their cats are safe from traffic, wild animals, or fighting with other cats, so they'll keep them indoors all the time. However, there are people and cultures who believe that it's animal cruelty to force cats to stay indoors and that they should have outdoor access, so they let them out during the day. One way or another, neither are wrong; it's a personal preference in what you believe will keep your cat safe and happy. Allow me to share a few conversations I've had with an indoor only cat, an outdoor-only cat, and a cat who lives both indoors and outdoors.

Perspective of an Indoor Cat, Butter

"There are times I wish I could go outside. However, outside seems really scary to me. There are cars on the road, people walking on the streets. I could get snatched up. I can hide, but then what's the point of enjoying the outdoors if you're going to hide all the time you're out there? I think being outside is overrated. I can see everything from the windowsill and hear the birds chirping away. I don't need to chase them, I don't really want to kill them, maybe just play with them, but then again, I'd have to go outside for that, and I just don't want to. At least when I'm indoors, I know I'm safe, I'm warm, I've got food and water whenever I want it. I'm taken care of, but if I go outside and I want to come in, who is going to open the door when I want to come in? What if they left the house when I'm still outside?

"Regarding fresh air, my humans keep the windows open in warmer weather, I don't need to go outside for that. Plus, who wants cold fresh air in the winter? I have warm beds to sleep in, especially when there's a lovely sunbeam. You can't have comfort and a sunbeam when you're outdoors. Being indoors means I get to live longer. I don't get into as many accidents as I would if I was outdoors. I don't get into cat fights. I don't get hurt as much. I'm much safer because I'm an indoor cat."

When I asked him if he misses hunting, smelling the earth and the grass Butter replied:

> *"Why do I need to hunt? I don't want to kill anything. I can stimulate my mind by playing with my brother and stalking him. I can smell the earth in the potted plants in the home. I tell ya, I've got it made being an indoor cat; I'm not missing much."*

Perspective from an indoor and outdoor cat, Rowley

I met Rowley in 2014 at the Vancouver Orphan Kitten Rescue Association (VOKRA) where I volunteered my time talking with the animals and answering any questions the volunteers and staff may have for specific animals. Rowley was in the feral section of VOKRA, and it was here where he told me his name was Rowley. He's since transitioned out of his body; however, he had a lot to say on what it was like to be an indoor and outdoor cat.

> *"I was able to go out in the mornings, but I had to come home by a particular time at night depending on the season. If it was winter, I had to be home before the sun went down, and if it was summer, I was able to stay out until 10:00 at night. I pushed the curfew a lot and Mum was never happy about it. She and Dad always worried as to whether I would be safe and healthy when I came back.*
>
> *"I have to admit, though, there were times I didn't come back for days, and that's when Mum would get you to talk with me. I didn't like coming home because*

it meant I would be in the house for hours on end. I only really came home to spend time with my family, to get fed, and to rest. I would sleep outside, but I also knew it wasn't all that safe so I would find a bush that I would sleep underneath to keep me as safe as I possibly could. I left because I got pissed off at Mum, Dad, or the dog, so I'd say, 'screw you—I'm outta here, and see if you like it when I'm gone!

"There was one time when my mum didn't let me out of the house for over a day because she had to take me in to see the veterinarian's, something to do with my health, who knows what it was about, but I wasn't happy, so I took off when I got home and didn't come back for a week. That's when you'd get involved, Karen. Mum would call you and then we'd negotiate as to when I'd be willing to come home, which would be in a few days, but Mum and Dad never liked that at all. They got scared and I can't say I couldn't blame them at all. I'd get scared for them when they'd just take off without telling me so I can't blame them when I'd do the same to them.

"I liked being an indoor cat when it poured rain here in Vancouver. I hated the rain and the sensation it felt on my fur when it would pour down on me. I just hated that feeling. I loved being home when I got fed because I could go to sleep afterwards knowing I was safe. I also loved being home because I could cuddle up with my humans to show them love but also to keep warm. I didn't mind the food that my parents gave me, but I liked the food I could find outside better. I was able to

catch mice and birds; they were always yummy. I also ate human food on the streets, but that was not so great for my digestion; I didn't like the way it made me feel. If I couldn't find enough birds or mice, that's when I would usually go home to get food. I had the best of both worlds, the comforts of being home but also the adventures of being an outdoor cat."

Reflections from an outdoor-only cat, Pepper

Pepper is a rescued, working barn cat who is now living a great life on a farm in Florida. When I asked Pepper what it's like living outside of the house full time this is what she had to say:

"I've got a great life living outside all the time. The weather can get cold, but that's what fur is for, isn't it? My fur keeps me warm, especially in winter. My job is to keep the farm's rat population down; they're a real nuisance. They get into the chicken's feed. They poop everywhere, which is just nasty. At least I have a litter box that my mum cleans out all the time for us. (She's referring to her adopted sister cat, Smoke). They're just filthy creatures and they don't taste very good, either.

"I love prey food; I love my meat raw, however, rats just don't taste good, I prefer birds. I don't eat the chicken or the peacocks, those are our friends, they belong here on the farm, so it's my job to make sure that everyone remains healthy by killing the rats.

"I live in the barn with my adopted sister, Smoke. I can come in and out whenever I want to, but if I was living in my mum's home it'd be very restrictive. I'd

have to depend on someone to open the door for me and I could only go out at certain times. I don't think I was meant to be an indoor cat at all. At least I have the full roam of the farm. I know better than to go out to the surrounding forest. Our mum can't keep us safe if we go out wandering there. At least in the barn and on the farm, I have freedom and safety. I keep the place really clean from rats. I'm fed, watered, littered and I can come and go as I please. My mum is very attentive to all of the animals' needs. I just can't imagine living in such a constrained situation where I don't have any free will to come and go when I want.

"I'd consider myself a semi-feral cat; I'm friendly with my mum, I love her to bits, however, if a stranger or a person I don't know well comes close to me, I'd get outta there like a flash. I love the fresh air, I love the smells all around me, in the air and the earth. When I'm smelling for rats on the ground, I can also smell which animal on the farm is ill or isn't feeling well. I know there isn't any way that I can tell my mum there's a particular animal who isn't well, but I do give that animal extra loving attention and energy which seems to help them until mum figures it out and attends to their needs. I guess you could consider me the first-aid responder of the farm. If I were an indoor cat I couldn't help the sick animals. I wouldn't be able to figure out who needed my help. Ugh—just the thought of living in a house makes me want to gag."

Bird cages—freedom or restriction?

When I first telepathically connected with Einstein a few years ago, I wanted to hear his experience of what it's like to live in a cage rather than having free roam of the house and/or living outside. In our conversation, he shared:

> *"I love my cage. People may think that birds don't like living in cages but that's not necessarily true. I find my cage to be quite comforting as it's my 'home' inside my larger home. When I want to have time to myself, I enjoy being in my cage. I get let out once in a while, and I don't mind that but for the most part I really enjoy being inside my cage. I do feel comforted and safe being in my bird home. That's what I like to call it, my bird home. I have my toys, my food, I feel warm, what more could I ask for? I know my family loves me; they pay attention to me, they tell me I'm really pretty, that I'm a 'pretty bird'; I know I am. I see myself in the mirror. I can watch the whole family and everything that's going on from my bird home. I highly recommend that if people want birds, they should go get them. I'm sure they'd feel the same way as I do about my bird home."*

In that same conversation, I specifically asked him, what do you think about people thinking that it's cruel for birds to live in cages, that they should be free to fly? His response:

> *"I can fly in the house if I want to. I'm safe but, my goodness, if it wasn't for my bird home, I wouldn't be safe. The birds outside are meant to be outside; they're*

wild, they are the ones that aren't meant to be in cages, those who have to fly freely. They soar in the air. Do I wish I could do that? Sometimes, but not often—that's a very scary thought, and I don't know if I'd be able to find my way back home, and I love my humans. They're important to me.

"I think I'd like to feel what it would be like to have wind going through my feathers but again, I think it'd be too scary for me. I'd probably be lunch for a larger bird; I've seen it happen when I look outside. I sing. I make my humans laugh. I'm loved. What more could I possibly want?

"So, there are plenty of birds who probably need homes, so why not give them a home? Bird homes, or in what you consider cages, aren't cruel; they're my safe space. I hope it changes people's minds about having a bird and thinking of it in a different way, that's all."

Shortly after talking with him, he transitioned out of his body. It was almost as if he were waiting for us to have this conversation before he left his body.

Asking permission from our animals

As humans, we often force ourselves upon our animals without their consent. We assume they always want to be petted or out on a walk (such as with dogs); we allow others to come up to them and pet them. In the case of horses or animals we ride, we get on their backs. All these behaviors are often without taking our animals' cues or spending the time to try to communicate with them about whether they're interested in our physical advances. This is very annoying and sometimes upsetting to our animals. It's important we ask for their consent and help to create boundaries for other humans who are reaching in for the pet, hug, squeeze, etc.

I asked Nacho, my friend Naomi's dog, for his perspective on what it's like to be walking with his humans when strangers come up to pat him. Nacho is usually a friendly dog who likes people's attention; however, there are times when he doesn't want anyone touching him. Here's what Nacho has to say in his own words:

> *"The message I'd like to tell people is that they need to be respectful of the dogs. Not all of us want to be petted; not all of us want attention no matter how 'cute' or 'adorable' we are. Sometimes, I'm in a bad mood and I just want to be left alone when I'm on my walk with my human(s).*
>
> *"We're not objects, we're beings who are highly intelligent and know and understand more than what humans give us credit for. We're not objects that we're owned, we're living, breathing sentient beings who have our own preferences, wants, desires. So, please, next time when you're wanting to pet a dog, ask permission, not just from the human but also from us. Just because we smell your hand when you offer it to us doesn't mean that we want you to pet us. Just ask us out loud and if we turn our heads away, then please leave us alone.*
>
> *"We're not public property to be touched and patted just because our humans say you can; it doesn't mean that we want to be. I think that's the biggest message I can*

give to people. Just because our humans say 'yes, he is friendly, you can pat him' doesn't necessarily mean we want to be patted. I think this is the biggest complaint most dogs have of humans; they don't directly ask us permission to pat us, so listen to our body language."

An example of the animals using their body language to communicate "no" would be when they turn their heads and/or their bodies away or when they back away from you.

Horses have similar perspectives when it comes to being ridden. Asking for permission is a sign we respect them and even though a riding lesson might be scheduled for a certain day or time doesn't mean the horse wants to be ridden at that moment. Here's one horse, Codi's, explanation:

"When you ride us, make sure you're listening to what we have to say. We don't have the ability to speak with a voice box and create words as humans do, but we do have ways to communicate with not only one another but also with our humans and those around us. We get dismissed all of the time because we don't have the ability to voice our opinions. We can only do it through our body language, through our actions, through our temperament, and sometimes we're misunderstood about what we're trying to say to the humans.

"I would like people to know that it would be appreciated if they get out of their heads and stop thinking and start feeling with their hearts to understand and know what our needs are, what our preferences are, what our likes and dislikes are. Maybe we don't want to go for a

ride; even though it may be necessary for your schedule, maybe it's not okay on ours, more specifically, mine. Have you ever thought about getting permission to ride instead of just telling us we're going to be ridden?"

I asked Codi to be more specific: Why is asking permission important to you Codi?

"It's a matter of respect, treating us as equals, understanding that we are on the same level of equality. We were created by the Divine just as humans are, neither one is better nor worse, but humans have a sense of entitlement that is unjust.

"Don't get me wrong, I enjoy what I do, and I love having my person on my back. It's a dance we get to create together, whether it's just riding for the sake of being together or it's jumping and training for exhibitions. I believe though it's a matter of respecting us as equals. The recognition of us as being equals to humans.

"When we show our displeasure, we get yelled at, anger or frustration aimed at us, or sometimes we're swatted with that dreadful stick (crop). Just because you want something to happen doesn't mean that we're up for it. Listen and read our body language to determine whether we want to be ridden or not.

"I just feel we're disregarded a lot of the time for the rider's pleasure. Yes, I enjoy the exercise. Yes, I enjoy being active and having a partnership but some days I'm feeling off and need to rest. This is why, every day,

check in with your horse, ask for permission to ride, ask if the horse wants to be ridden and then be still, listen, watch, tune into your instincts because we will immediately tell you the answer. Nine times out of ten we will say yes, but it's the one time that gets overridden that it's not pleasant for anyone.

"Be kind, be courteous, treat us as you would like to be treated yourself, with dignity and respect. That is all."

In a separate instance many years ago involving a friend's horse, Sassy, Sassy went missing at an exhibition in La Quinta, California. I got a frantic call from my friend, Karen. I was in Naples, Florida at the time visiting my father and my bonus-mum when I got the call. Karen wanted me to track Sassy down. There were over 2,000 horses on the showgrounds, so you can imagine how big the property was! Now, normally I do not help to locate, track, or find lost or stolen animals, however, everyone was in a panic, and I thought I'd give it a shot. Plus, it was for my girlfriend.

As it turned out when I connected to Sassy, she told me that one of the groomers didn't fully shut her stall, so she took full advantage, let herself out, and found another stall far away from where her team was. When I asked her why she left, she explained that her human was talking about selling her in California and she didn't want to be sold in California, she wanted to go back up to British Columbia. She continued to explain that she didn't mind getting sold because she didn't really like jumping anyway and would prefer to dance, meaning dressage, but she wanted to be in British Columbia.

When I told her that I would talk to her human about her preferences, I asked her if she would show me where she hid herself. She described a specific stall, on the other side of the field and I was able to convey specific information to her human as to her location. When I told her human why and how she left her stall, not only did she find her, but she also told me that she was in fact talking about selling Sassy in California. She agreed she'd wait until she got back home to sell her. Fast forward the story—Sassy was sold to a dressage rider, and she excelled in her dancing!

This is an example of overlooking our animals' needs, preferences, or ideas, assuming we know what's best without considering their thoughts and feelings and why we shouldn't do it.

Muzzling

One last topic which warrants discussion is how muzzles on dogs are an important tool to use to ensure both humans' and animals' safety. The interesting part about this topic is how many dogs ask their humans to put the muzzles on them. We, as a society, have preconceived notions about what it means when we see a person walking with their dog who has a muzzle on. We immediately think "that dog is dangerous, we need to avoid him/her." We tend to think it was the human who made the decision to put a muzzle on their dog. However, how would our perception change if we knew that, in fact, it was the dog who requested to have the muzzle on? This is exactly what happened with my dog client, Dragon.

Dragon has a lack of impulse control. Her human came to me because her dog was so reactive it was becoming dangerous for other people to take care of her or to walk her. During one of our communication sessions, Dragon explained to her mum that she didn't trust herself enough to not bite or be reactive to people or other dogs. She said it doesn't take much for her to be reactive. Dragon then showed me a picture of what happens in her brain when she becomes triggered and reactive.

The best way I can describe it is the wiring in her brain is crossed. A spark gets ignited, and her reasoning rational mind gets shut down, (like a circuit breaker getting turned off), while the circuit breaker for the short wiring is on full throttle. There was no amount of medication, conventional and alternative, that could calm this dog's brain down. Dragon explained to her mum that she loves her life, she loves her, but she just couldn't trust herself to keep other people safe. She specifically asked her mum to please put a muzzle on her so she could relax when she went on walks and didn't have to worry about her brain being triggered and potentially biting someone or another dog. She explained she just wanted to enjoy herself when going on walks.

Her human had to really grapple with this notion of putting her dog on a muzzle because she believed she was being cruel to her dog. It took a few conversations between my client and Dragon for my client to fully understand that it wasn't cruel, it was what Dragon wanted. My client reported that since those conversations took place, putting a muzzle on Dragon made their walks easy and stress-free for both her and Dragon.

This conversation with Dragon truly turned my perspective around because whenever I see a muzzle on a dog, I quietly say to myself, "that's awesome, good for them and I bet they're having such a great stress-free walk." So, I encourage anyone who is grappling with the idea of needing to put a muzzle on their beloved dog, remember this conversation with Dragon;

see it as a positive tool that will alleviate worry, stress, and allow for more relaxed and happy walks.

Our animals deserve the same respect we desire, which means considering their safety as much as our own. Safety can look like keeping our animals inside or in a crate or cage or it can look like muzzling them on a walk. A part of safety is also consent and getting an animal's permission to pet them, ride them, put them in the car, et cetera. To understand each of our animal's boundaries, we need to open ourselves up to letting them guide us.

CHAPTER 6

RELATIONSHIPS AND FAMILY DYNAMICS

L ike humans, most animals are conscious beings who need and prefer the company and community of others versus going through life solo. We see proof of this repeatedly throughout the animal kingdom in the way several species stay together. Just think about all the names there are for the groups animals live in! Herd, pride, pack, pod, murder, gaggle, parliament, aggregation, crash, skulk, thunder…yes, all of these are real terms for communities of animals. Even if some species eventually leave "the nest," they mate (some for life), recreate, and rear their young for some portion of time. Given what Trick has taught us about the oversoul and oneness, the group culture that animal species create makes sense; they have a herd mind which interconnects them.

For our more domesticated animal friends who grace our homes, our family system, (including the humans and other animals in it), become their community or group. There's less universal oneness or oversoul when it comes to interspecies homes, but even if we can't communicate telepathically with one another, we are all still relating to and interacting with one another. What we do and say impacts those who live with us, including our animals. They feel and read our energy and that of the other animals in the house. They know when they are loved or welcomed and when they're not. They can sense when trouble is brewing at home between people or when their environment isn't safe. There's a lot they have to say about their relationships with humans and other animals which I'll relay in this chapter.

Matters of Adoption

Like children without parents, animals without homes need loving and reliable caregivers. Also, like children, not just the babies or the healthy ones are the ones needing adoption. There are older animals or animals with special needs who need homes and loving humans. When put in the right home, many of these animals thrive and feel they've found their 'forever home.' That said, it's important to take adoption seriously.

As Astrea (Naomi's dog) cautions: *"It's not something that you just go on a whim. You're responsible for another living being and it plays an emotional part on the animal. It's hard going from your first home of abuse into a shelter, and you have no idea what's going to happen to you. So, my message to humans about adopting an animal is to be very confident and sure of your decision because it's hard on our emotions if you end up sending us back because it's not what you expected. When you adopt, you're adopting for life. If you come from an abused home and you get adopted into a loving family like I did, it helps the emotional and mental wounds heal so much faster and you get to know what real and true love is like."*

All words of advice and wisdom aside, Astrea, loves being adopted.

> *"Being adopted is the best! It's like winning the lottery because the people who adopt you actually WANT you!! They don't yell at you, they don't get angry with you. My humans get stern and firm but that's because they want to make sure I'm safe, that I don't do anything stupid or that I don't ruin something that they love.*
>
> *"It's like knowing that you never, ever have to ever leave; you're never going to be sent away again. It's a really great feeling and knowing that I'm finally in my forever home and it doesn't matter what I do, I mean within reason, that they won't ever kick me out. I wasn't a puppy when I came to them, I was fully grown with a really bad history prior to my now family.*
>
> *"At first, I didn't know what to expect, so I was still tentative and scared. I didn't settle down immediately. I think it took me a couple of weeks to really figure out that I'm not going anywhere. It's the best feeling to know that I'm wanted and loved, and they'll do anything for me right now. "*

Remember, too, that animals pick their humans, and each animal has something to teach their human. This is no different when it comes to adoption. Here's Naomi's dad's dog Hale's story:

> *"I go everywhere with my human; I get to be a full-time companion and serve him in this way. I love my mum,*

don't get me wrong, but my dad needs me, and I fill his heart where it was sad and empty before. He lights up when I walk into the room and that fills my heart up. We were two lost souls needing each other without ever knowing we needed one another. I can run and play without the responsibilities of being a human, I get to be with other dogs, sleep when I want to, do whatever I want when I want, and nobody ever tells me differently. I get to rest, and I found my forever home. I wouldn't give it up for anything. I'm home. If you're ever considering adopting a dog, consider adopting an older dog who needs a chance. There are plenty of them on the street who need help. Everybody wants puppies, but I tell ya, older dogs need help, too, and we can make really good/great companions.

Animals who are adopted into safe and loving homes often prefer it over a life living on the street as strays. While there may be certain freedoms, being able to go wherever an animal may like to roam, living as a stray also comes with the uncertainty of where they'll find food or shelter or whether they'll survive other natural elements like weather, illness, or other animals.

Hale does a wonderful job describing what it was like living on the streets versus living in a home. We know that before he was found he and his sister were dumped in a ditch and was in foster care for several years because no one wanted him.

This is what Hale has to say about being adopted into a forever home:

"I don't have to take care of myself. There are people who love me that do that for me. I don't have to wonder

where my next meal is going to be; I love being adopted and having a home. I don't have to worry about where I'm going to keep warm, where I'm going to sleep that's safe, if I'm even going to be able to sleep because I don't want to be attacked by a bigger dog or worse, a predator who is looking for food. I've had plenty of experiences of not being able to sleep fully, always being alert, one eye open so to speak, not getting the rest I need. I always had to look for my food; it wasn't fun.

"The best thing about being adopted is that I have a loving home, a warm fireplace in winter, and food that's automatically given to me; I don't even have to beg for it, it just arrives. I get all the pats and love I want. It's truly the best being adopted into a loving home. I wish that all the street cats and dogs, or any animal for that matter, would get adopted into a safe, loving home like mine."

Animal shelters everywhere are overrun with rescued animals looking for tender-hearted humans who will be patient and kind and give them a chance. Some of these animals have been rescued from the streets where they've endured harsh survival conditions. They have had to find their own shelter from natural elements and their own food sources, which are not guaranteed, avoid being hit by any number of vehicles, and endure lack of medical care when they're in need. These animals have as much to give us as a purebred pup or horse or a friendly barn cat that just birthed a litter of kittens, but may require the right home, care, and patience as they may not be immediately trusting of humans.

As one feral cat, Rowley, explains, "*Be patient with feral cats, we're worth it. Have patience with us. We don't like living on the streets; it's mean and hard. We're in a constant state of survival. Remember, when you adopt a feral cat, it'll be work. Be patient no matter how many years it'll take for us to connect with you. Just know that we appreciate you taking a chance on us and one day we'll show you how much even if it's just sitting in the same room as you. Having no expectations of us gives us permission to take our time to trust. Love goes a long way. We may not show it but we certain feel it and appreciate it.*"

Feral and stray animals aren't the only ones taken in by shelters and awaiting good homes. Other animals are rescued from mills or other abusive residences, or homes where a human family member has died and there's no surviving family members to take them, or other living situations that are unhealthy for animals, such as Curious's experience living in a hoarder's home before being rescued.

Curious, her biological sister Tenderfoot, and three other siblings, lived in a hoarder's house, with twenty-seven other cats when they were kittens. She remembers the conditions and how hard her mum cat worked to keep her and her siblings safe. She remembers being rescued and the day I adopted her along with Tenderfoot. This is how she tells it:

> "*It was horrible. We couldn't breathe well. Tenderfoot and I were the sickest, even though I was the largest and felt responsible for the other kittens. Our mother did a great job protecting us and getting what little food she could find for us. There was never enough food, and we had to share what little there was. There were too many cats in the home; a lot of them were mean. We*

weren't happy, the house smelled gross—mouldy, dirty, dusty, musty, urine smells. Overall, it was just terrible. We lived in that place for nine weeks. I never thought it would end I thought we would be living there for the rest of our lives! It was my mum cat who protected us enough to make sure we survived, even though Tenderfoot and I were sick. The other three kittens were strong and didn't get sick. Mum didn't let us wander off; she would always pull us back into our little corner of the house.

"I remember the day we were rescued pretty clearly. It was scary, I have to admit. I was separated from my mum and a few of my siblings. We didn't know what was happening; there was a lot of confusion. I settled down once we were together again. We were put into a kennel together, and we stayed there until we got a bit better and then our human came to pick us up.

"It was scary; I didn't know what was going to happen with us. We were separated from our mother for the first time, it was just the five of us and that's it. When I was put into the bathroom where you kept us for a few days, I realized that we were going to be fed multiple times a day, that food was always coming, that our litters were always going to be cleaned. I never had that before. I became more relaxed and settled over the next couple of weeks trusting you and Dad. We began to play again with each other at night, especially because that was when it was the quietest. Tenderfoot wasn't in good shape, and we didn't know if she was going to make it or not."

As Curious and Tenderfoot's story illustrates, compromised animals want a chance at being adopted, too. Both were sickly because of the conditions they were born into and required extra care. In another cat's instance, they were deaf, blind, and lived with a neurological condition... that cat's name was Beamer. Beamer shares, *"Adopt the compromised animals. You'll be rewarded beyond your wildest dreams…we may be disabled or restricted in some areas, but we'll teach you to relate to us in different ways that you never thought possible. Your heart will expand exponentially."*

Another matter of adoption to consider is whether to adopt more than one animal at a time, especially when siblings are concerned, and they've never been separated or when there are no other cats in the home. Deirdre's cat, Peanut, thinks it's important to adopt two cats together:

> *"It's important that you adopt two cats together. I'm lucky enough that I got adopted with my brother, Butter. We've been together since we were born, and we've never been separated. We've been there for one another when we get scared. Like when the kids get really loud, a loud voice is being used, or there's yelling—that sort of thing. It just gets a bit scary, and my brother is there for me and I'm there for him.*

> *"I can't imagine not being with another cat sharing my life with, especially my brother. We can sleep together when we get chilled; we keep each other warm and toasty. It's comforting to have one another when we get nervous; we groom each other in those hard-to-reach places, or the places that we can't even reach like the*

nape of our necks, top of our heads, back of our ears. (Paws sometimes just don't do it, so a good tongue licking is exactly what's needed—it's like scratching pad that feels soooo good!) We play with each other, not so much now as we're grown-up adult cats, but when we were younger, boy did we play with each other, and we had so much fun! I think it would be really lonely not to be living with another cat.

"I do live with a dog, but it's not the same; his tongue isn't scratchy. He doesn't understand cat culture well. I mean, it's nice to know he's around, but really, it's only living with another cat that makes me feel fully understood. I don't have to explain myself; I just am. I get to just be.

"So, when people are considering adoption, please make sure it's with two cats. They don't have to be from the same litter, just make sure that there are two. When our family members aren't home, at least I know I've got company if I need it. I just don't think it's fair that people will only adopt one cat—that can get really lonely."

Multi-animal homes

Most of my clients have a multi-animal home, and oftentimes questions revolve around the relationships between and amongst all the animals. For example, problems can range from an animal guarding resources, such as food and water, to not allowing other animals to walk down a hallway or go up the stairs. There can be many reasons for this behavior, but as long as it remains unaddressed by humans, the behaviour will continue, and over time, the dynamics will get worse amongst the animals. Unfortunately, it's usually when an animal gets hurt in a fight, trying to retaliate against the animal who is guarding, when the human finally notices that things aren't all right between the animals. Just like in most homes, family members get along but not all the time; the same happens with animals. The following are examples of how animals experience living in multi-animal households.

Multi-cat relationships

Not all cats are like Peanut and enjoy living with other cats (or other animals in general). Scrunchy (also a cat), says, *"There are a lot of different personalities, and you have to figure out what each one likes and doesn't like and adhere to that. Be respectful, mindful. We learn to live with each other even though sometimes the circumstances aren't ideal."* Since then, I've spoken more with Scrunchy and asked her for clarity and to elaborate.

To paraphrase, when you're living in a home with multiple cats, some will be more like frenemies and others like best friends. Some will irritate you and others are your sidekicks. She identified one cat as being like her little brother, another like her mum, and a third as a cat she just likes to hang and sleep with, while others get on her nerves. Here's what she said specifically:

> *"It's like living with your best friends for life. You can depend on them; you've got a friend who will lick in the hard-to-reach places that you can never get at, and they'll lick it for you. You've got a warm body to curl into and sleep, keeping you safe and warm. Sometimes it's like living with your siblings—you fight, ignore, don't have anything to do with one another, but you're*

glad they're around in case, on the off chance, you need them."

Even with the possibility of conflict or the challenge of living with other animals, Scrunchy says she'd never want to live on her own with humans.

"It'd be too lonely; the humans don't understand cat language and culture. They're lovely; I love my humans very much, but I need my cat friends. They're a great comfort to me."

Another thing that humans may not be aware of is that multi-cat systems have an alpha just like canine packs. Lots of cats in the home operate like a big-cat pride (think about lions with a male as the alpha of the pride) but on a smaller scale, as Umbra (Naomi's cat) has shared with me. If you have more than one cat living in the home, likely one is playing the role of the alpha and the other cats are looking to it for wisdom, guidance, and conflict resolution. The cats choose the alpha and the alpha not only mediates between the other cats but ensures keeping the peace for the greater family system. Here's how Umbra describes it:

"Cats need a sense of leadership; it's in our DNA, it's in our culture…it's a lot of responsibility to be the alpha cat, always having to manage the other cats' behaviors and dynamics amongst each other. The complaints that they have about one another is just so tiresome and petty—who hissed at who first…who is playing with another's toy even though it belongs to everyone, who

is sleeping in their spot… Most of the time I roll my eyes and just tell them to figure it out amongst themselves. I just ignore them. I don't want to be in this position, but if it becomes a more serious matter, like who is intentionally bugging another cat in the pride, way past the initial hiss, then I'll step in because they're not respecting one another's boundaries. Sometimes, the other cats don't want to be bothered and are pushovers, so I'll step in. I'll step in if I think a hissing for warning will turn into a bite or something more serious like a full-on rough and tumble fight.

"This home is calm; it's loving, and I really hate it when there's rough and tumble fighting and it's not playful. That's not okay. The younger cats will usually work things out amongst themselves, but if it gets out of control then that's when I've got to play parent, even though I don't want to. I just want to be left alone. I've got to step in and tell them to knock it off and then order is usually restored. If I didn't intervene, all hell would break loose, there wouldn't be any order, resentments would build, anger would rise, there would be constant fighting, bullying, intimidating, and energy blocking from resources of food and water.

"If I didn't step in, it would cause a lot of stress for Mum and Dad, and that's the last thing I want to see happening. They've been so good to us, and they love us so much; they don't deserve to be dealing with chaos amongst us. So, I love my parents so much that I've stepped into this role because the others are too young with not much wisdom behind them to be able to command a presence

of order and peace. I would say to humans that they need to trust their pride to figure out who will keep order in the bunch. If none appears, then be prepared for a lot of fighting and chaos amongst the cats."

Multi-species relationships and homes

Given some of the angst between cats, it's not hard to see that some cats might prefer being in homes with other animals, like dogs (or even birds, which I'll discuss soon). Despite believing cats and dogs are like oil and water, several I know have very special bonds. In fact, some would even say it's better than having the same species at home because there is less competition. Take my sister, Ainsley's, cat and dog, Honeybee and Blackjack, as an example. Honeybee enjoys having a dog as a friend versus another cat.

"We don't have to compete for resources such as food, water or litter...I can be relaxed around my dog. He's big but he's respectful of my size. We love cuddling up together; I think he tolerates me more than I him. We love lying with each other.

"Sometimes he gets a bit too rambunctious, and I have to run away to remind him he's bigger than I am, and I don't want him pounding on me. We share the same bed (our mum's bed that is), but we sleep quite closely to one another, keeping each other company through the night.

"He tells me all the adventures he goes on with our mum in the car. I hate the car because it means only one thing—the vet's. He tells me he goes everywhere

with Mum and describes all the different parks, trees, smells, water, the ocean, and sometimes he says he just goes with her to help her with the errands but just stays in the car. He doesn't understand the point of doing that, but he says at least he's with her. I love hearing about his adventures. I don't necessarily wish I could go with them but it's nice to hear what he says.

"I don't think I'd like another cat for a companion. There's no angst, there's no cat fighting, there's no competition. It's more relaxed. Having a dog for a companion works well for me. I wouldn't want it any other way. Life is good when you have a dog in it."

Blackjack shares his sentiments:

"Living with a cat is a lot of fun. I have to keep on my toes because sometimes she'll just swat me for no reason. I wouldn't want to live with another dog—that'd take too much of my mum's attention away from me." He admits they like to share the bed together but not in a curled-up way. "We'll sleep on the bed together with our backs touching."

That said, he does find it difficult sometimes to play with her. He must watch his size and weight because he's so much bigger than her and he says their mum is "always telling me to be gentle." Blackjack also says HB's claws are sharp. "They can dig right into my fur, but she does her best not to hurt me."

Earlier in the book, we introduced Nacho and Einstein who also live with a cat, Purrfect. They found a certain harmony in living with each other. Purrfect says, "We've learned to respect one another. We've known each other for so long honestly, it's no biggie." Admittedly, she doesn't see Nacho as her best friend and rather he'd play with other dogs, but when I asked her if she would want to live with other cats, she echoed what Honeybee had to say. "No, I don't think I would. I'd be competing for attention and play time."

Now, if cats and dogs can thrive living together, then so can other animal species we might otherwise assume wouldn't get along, such as cats and birds. We have assumptions that cats eat birds, but when living together in a family system, these animals are family members more than predator and prey. I took the opportunity to ask Purrfect her thoughts on living with other species different from her, such as the dog and bird she lives with.

"The bird is a lot of fun; I'm not allowed to go near him, but I don't mind. It's not like I'm going to hurt him. He's very entertaining and makes my humans laugh. I love watching him. He's very flitty and moves quickly so his movements always catch my eyes. I pretend I'm going to prey on him; I get a whole imaginary world in my mind about pouncing on him and playing with him. But would I eat him? No way! He's part of the family. I just would like to be given the chance to play with him, but I think my humans are too afraid that I would do damage to him with my claws. I can't say I blame them. He has a very pretty voice but sometimes it gets on my nerves. There's only so much chirping a cat can handle."

Perhaps the most notable thing to take away from these animals' insights about living with different species in the home is that each species has their own culture with their own rules and boundaries. As Purffect puts it, "When we come together, we exchange information. We set the parameters and boundaries and then we can live harmoniously together."

Human/animal relationships, dynamics, and bonds

The human-animal bond is so intermingled, it's intangible—deeply felt between the animal and its human. This bond impacts one another to the degree that humans will make life-changing decisions based on their animals' needs.

For example, I had a client, Tricia, whose two cats kept hiding in the bedroom closet and wouldn't come out. Sophie was very concerned for her cats, so she connected with me to have a conversation with her about their hiding. There was one cat who spoke for both of them, Sophie. Now, remember, I never edit what the animals say; it's not my conversation. I am literally just the telephone, and telephones don't edit what's said.

Sophie came out in full swing yelling at her mother in anger for tolerating Tricia's husband's verbal and emotional abuse. He was a long-haul truck driver, so he spent many weeks on the road; they would come out of the closet every time he left but went back in when he came home.

Sophie swore at her mother because the anger was so intense, and she needed to get her point across that it was just as abusive to her and her sister when they were watching their mother get screamed at. When they shared their thoughts with me, they were so angry, they used expletives and called her selfish for subjecting them to abuse. They also explained to her that they either wanted to be rehomed so they didn't have to be subjected to that and continue to be traumatized OR they wanted her to move out of the house, take them, and leave him. Tricia was crying as she apologized and told them she'd seriously take into consideration everything they said in making her decision.

I received a call three months later from Tricia explaining that even though many of her family members and friends kept urging her to leave her husband out of concern for her, she took everything her cats said into consideration and, even though she wasn't in the position to leave her husband entirely, she realized they needed help, so she sought the support needed to do the inner work and change her reactions to what was happening. While healing, for her, is still a process, she said her cats literally saved her life. She said not only is her life now much better, but the cats are no longer hiding and are spending their days and nights with her.

This is such a great example of how impactful and deep the relationship between animals and their humans can get. It's amazing how it took an honest conversation with her cats to finally get the necessary help she needed to make significant changes in her life. Sometimes it really does take the love of our animals to make some of the hardest decisions we've ever had to make.

The same can happen when joy, excitement, elation, love, and gratitude happens for the human; it also can happen for their animal. The animal feeds off the positive energy from their human and their human then feels their animal's joy that it becomes a self-feeding upward spiral.

Transitions and Separation Anxiety

My biggest concern that my clients have for their cats is peeing outside of the litter box, and for those who have dogs, it is separation anxiety. I always make sure that my clients have taken their animals to their veterinarians first to determine if these behaviors are due to physical issues that need medical attention. Once it's been determined by the vet that they're physically fine, we can have a conversation with the animals.

What I've learned over the years from cats is they pee outside of the box, and even sometimes on the bed, because they're literally "pissed off." It's usually due to a few main reasons, life transitions such as a new baby, a new animal, a death in the family or an animal friend, a move, or divorce.

For example, a client and her husband contacted me because her cat, let's call her Magic, refused to pee inside the litter box. Magic seemed tense and nervous all the time; she wouldn't play and interact with her humans. When I connected with Magic, she immediately told me she was upset because her parents were talking about separating and she didn't know who she would live with. She said she'd like to stay with her mother.

Before I relayed this information to Magic's humans, I asked them if they could scoot the children out of the room because I didn't know whether the children knew their parents were talking about separating. Once the kids were out of earshot, I told them exactly what Magic wanted to tell them. They were so surprised, they asked me how I knew they were talking about separating. I told them I didn't know; Magic told me.

Other reasons cats might pee outside the litter box are because they don't like the litter box and/or the type of litter used. Once we've determined what they're unhappy about, the acting out usually resolves if their humans follow through with agreements made with their cats.

Regarding dogs and separation anxiety, this usually results from either physical or verbal abuse or trauma from being a street dog, tension in the house, stress and tension within their humans, or the dogs' stressful in utero experience. It could also be that they've carried a past life over to this present life that needs to be healed. Some of the ways to alleviate the anxiety is to make sure you tell your animals what time you'll be back, who you're going to be with, and where you're going. Also, put some clothes with your scent on them in their bed so they can smell you until you come home.

The animals in our homes are as much a part of our human family system as they are a part of their animal family, community, or group. In some ways more if their contact or connection with other animals is absent or they aren't experiencing the oneness or oversoul with others of their kind. As such, we must be mindful of the way we interact, relate, and engage with the other human members of our family and the animals themselves since they feel and read our energy and that of the others in the home. They know when they are loved and welcomed. They know when there is stress and tension. They feel well beyond our understanding. They bond to us as deeply as we bond to them.

PART 3

Animal Wisdom and Messages About Death, Dying, and the Afterlife

CHAPTER 7

DEATH, DYING, AND CHOOSING WHEN TO LEAVE THEIR BODY

I'm sure we've all wondered what happens after we die and what happens to our animals once they die. This next part of the book is about the animals' perspective and experience with death, the transition from being in their body to leaving their body, and what happens in spirit. Is there a heaven for animals? Are there ways for animals to visit humans even after death? These are all questions this chapter and the next few explore.

Perhaps the most important message animals wish to impart on us is that death is not to be feared and it's not forever. This can offer humans peace of mind and therefore gives animals peace of mind. Death needs to be normalized, which I believe our animals' messages and wisdom can help us to do if more of us become attuned to them. Animals see death as a cycle, as the part of life when the physical form ends and a new state of being begins. They have an inner knowing that life in a physical form is only a temporary thing.

When an animal dies, it gives us the opportunity to broaden our preconceived notions about dying and death and what it means. This is not to say that we shouldn't feel the pain of losing our animals, after all, we are human beings with emotions and a deep love for our animal companions and that must be valued and respected. We will, of course, go through the grieving process; this book isn't to dismiss the depth of heartache we feel when they die. However, we can use these opportunities to expand our understanding of death and what it means. It prompts us to ask those questions like: Is there life after death? Do we just stop existing or does our consciousness continue?

Death is a season and the experience like a tree

One day last winter, I was walking through the forest with my grand dog, Leo, noticing that as the snow was falling everything was much quieter. I watched Leo interact with the woods, being one with the energy as the forest itself goes to sleep. As we all know, it sleeps for a few months then the plants, trees, ferns, shrubs, and bushes awaken in the spring. Autumn is deceiving to the eyes in that it looks like the plants are dying as the leaves are falling and everything is turning brown, but what I noticed in that moment was that the trees, the bushes, and ferns go to sleep to rest and rejuvenate as they've had a long season of new growth. They must rest to be able to come back and produce more, which is a way for them to fully express themselves.

What happens with the leaves on the trees or the plants in the ground is essentially what happens to an animal's soul when it leaves the body. It's played hard, loved deeply, and was protected by the body which has done so much over its lifetime (perhaps with some scrapes, bumps, bruises, ACL tears, hips deteriorating, and sometimes broken limbs), and just like leaves on the trees need to "fall" and come back to earth, so does the physical form of an animal. They "shed their coat" so their soul can be released from its physical form.

Whether or not the animal's soul returns to another body or to the same human family doesn't really matter. What does matter is the soul and spirit of that animal continues to exist. Just as a tree, bush, or flower isn't dead simply because it hasn't blossomed or bud in the cold season, an animal's spirit doesn't die because its physical form has. The animal's body may no longer exist because the Soul no longer occupies it, but that doesn't mean the Soul stops living. The essence of the animal hasn't perished, just the physical form. The physical form is the illusion, and the soul/spirit of the animals is the reality.

Kaia offers this perspective: "You call it dying. I call it taking my coat off." The same way a tree sheds its leaves, an animal sheds its coat (scales, skin, fur, etc.)

> *"Humans believe that once we leave our bodies that's the end of our relationship. That's not the case. Just because you can't see us or feel us, doesn't mean we're gone. We're still around you, watching you, listening to you. Please continue to speak to us as if our physical bodies are still with you. We haven't left; we've just changed clothes."*

Just as the tree always exists, the animal spirits always exist. It's the leaves on the body of the tree that fall, not the tree itself. You can't see the roots, but you know they're underground, under the earth rejuvenating, collecting energy, going to sleep. You can't see the roots, but you know they exist. We can't see the souls or spirits of our animals, but they exist.

The energies of an animal are the same as the energies of the forest, the same as the energies of a human being, the same as the energies of all warm- and cold-blooded beings. We're all the same, just manifested in different forms. We are equal to each other and of each other while the energy swirls around and keeps that form of energy in place. This may be a bit esoteric, however this is what I see when I work with animals and it's the constant flow of energy in the consciousness and awareness that keeps that soul and spirit alive in form from one shape to another shape.

The gifts and offerings of death

Death allows us to reflect on the great times we had with our animal companions, to delve deep into the joy of having them, to remember the love that expanded in our hearts that grew when they were in our lives. Death is not the end, it's just another chapter of reality for both animals and their humans.

Death is necessary for the animal's soul's evolution. They've learned the lessons they needed to in their lifetime with their person; the same goes with the person having their animal in their life. Perhaps the humans learned how to expand their love bandwidth and to grow and deepen their ability to be compassionate and empathetic towards themselves, their animals, and other people. Perhaps the animal was a teacher for them in developing patience (I know my cats continually teach my husband and me a lot about this subject). Focusing on the animal's learning first—the animal knows when its "job" is complete, and its soul has expanded the way it was intended; it's learned what it was sent here to learn. At that point, the animal's soul remains until its predetermined time of transition is set to happen.

However, once they've left their physical form, they're still in a state of energy, awareness, knowledge, and understanding of what is happening around them. I'm being shown as I write this how they hover over their body taking everything in. In this moment, they're figuring out they've left their bodies. It's at this point in time we need to do the Crossing Over Prayer (Appendix A) for our animals' souls to ensure that they do cross over the rainbow bridge (which we'll discuss in Chapter 9).

Past lifetimes, future lifetimes, and soul contracts

A question I get asked frequently is, "Were my animals and I together in past lives? It feels as though we've known each other for a long time." Or "Will my animal come back to me in this lifetime?" Or "Will my animal and I have future lifetimes together?"

These are all reasonable questions, and it is only natural to want to know the answers. We love our animals so much that we'd love to know if we've had lifetimes together or if we will continue to have lifetimes together, and/or if they'll come back to us in our current lifetime. What I've come to learn from the animals after all these years of talking with them is that humans and animals create a soul contract between one another. The human agrees to have the animal in their life and the animal agrees to be in the human's life.

Now, the issue is what kind of animal will that soul enter into and what kind of circumstances need to exist for the arrival of that animal into the human's life? I'm going to use Naomi's cat, Persephone's, story to illustrate this point. Persephone shared with me that animals choose their people, not the other way around. When I asked her to tell me more, she shared her experience.

"I sent a message out to the ethers to my now-mum to let her know that I want to be with her, and she found me. We had a spirit contract to be together in this lifetime. It doesn't matter if people do or do not believe in past lifetimes or spirit contracts, they exist. So, my mum and I agreed prior to coming to this earth plane that we would be together in this lifetime. I put the message out in the ethers that I've been born and it's now time to pick me up and she did. I was with a litter of other kittens at a shelter; she found me on the computer and came and got me. I knew she would, and I'm so lucky that we're now together.

"I want people to know that the animals you have now in your life, you've had them in your lifetimes before this one. There's something comforting to know that we'll always be in each other's lives from one to the next. We each play a role for each other, teaching one another, being a companion for one another, loving each other, comforting each other from one lifetime to another and with each lifetime our bond grows. Sometimes new animals come onto the scene with a human, and it's a fresh, new relationship as the bond starts to grow between the two spirits. These animals bonded to their humans play such an important role in friendship, companionship, love, laughter, joy, tears, and upset. We're there for each other.

"So, what I want people to know is that when you sense that deep, special, one-of-a-kind bond with your animal or have that feeling with just one animal that you've had in your life, you know that's your companion who has been with you through multiple lifetimes, and they know you like they know the back of their

*paw. They know you inside and out, and that's a com-
forting feeling for the human."*

Soul contracts: choosing the circumstances of their death

In addition to choosing their human, the animal will also choose the circumstances of their death and dying experience. In other words, before the soul entered the animal's physical body, the animal decided how they would die and roughly when they would die. They'll even choose in advance who will be there (if at all) for their death, and what kind of illness or experience they'll have in order to leave their body. There are more of these principles to discuss in the upcoming chapters.

Soul contracts: choosing the lessons to be learned

Much of the time, the animal will choose to create its life circumstances where it's a learning experience for both them and their human. As Spirit once shared with me—and I'm paraphrasing—animals know exactly who they'll be with and who they'll help. They also know whether they'll be living on the streets, in a rescue, or in a home.

Their entire life path has been mapped out to include specific lessons they'll learn for their evolutionary and spiritual growth. They'll even choose to be in specific circumstances to understand or learn from these circumstances what they need to do for their higher good. For example, consider living on the streets or having a home. Here's something Spirit shared that I'm leaving intact because it was perfectly stated.

*"As humans, you have an understanding that it's awful
for animals who are living in the streets, however, one
must understand there is a rich environment in the*

streets of learning for that animal's soul. If they were meant to be rescued, then they will. Being rescued has the same value in learning as does living in the streets for their entire lives."

What humans don't seem to understand is that they, too, have a life-plan that's mapped out prior to being born onto the Earth's plane. They have things to learn and teach one another for their and each other's personal growth and evolution.

Curious explains the idea of choosing circumstances and lessons this way:

> *"My human, Karen, and I have a soul contract to be together in this lifetime. We committed to each other that we'd be there for one another no matter what circumstances arise in our lifetime together. In our particular contract, I agreed I would appear as a black cat, because black cats are powerful and psychic. We're able to protect our humans from dark energies. Everything that human beings say about black cats being bad luck is nonsense. In fact, we're the opposite of that.*

> *"In Karen's line of work, I help protect her and the animal she's either talking with or working on. I'm able to chase the negative entities away and keep the space she's working in free of dark beings. When Karen works, she needs all the protection she can get and what's more powerful than a black cat who's intelligent, psychic, and a sentient being such as myself?*

> *"Karen agreed to take care of me. I chose to be born into a compromised body to learn how to surrender, to*

trust that I will be taken care of, that my humans will attend to my needs and be concerned for my well-being. I needed to learn that it's not every lifetime I will be neglected or abused, but that I'll be loved and appreciated for who I am.

"I get frustrated with my body a lot; it doesn't work the way I want it to all the time, and I get really frustrated especially when my hind legs aren't working. They slip out from under me when I'm running around or chasing my sister, Tenderfoot, when we have the zoomies. My mum (Karen) and dad (Drummond), are there, with kind, loving words of understanding and compassion, and they tell me that I'm going to be fine no matter what happens with my body, and I believe them. Since I believe in them, I can be confident in who I am, surrender myself to the circumstances that I chose to be in my body, and allow their love to help me through the difficult times when I'm really frustrated.

"You see, this contract that we agreed upon is mutually beneficial. It's respectful, loving, and we are of service to one another."

Tenderfoot offers her own perspective on soul contracts as she shows me pictures of grass, weeds, flowers, stones, and rocks when she discusses other forms she may have previously been in:

"My soul contract is with both my mum and dad. I chose my dad, Drummond, because I needed to learn boundaries. I'm a newish soul. I've been in different forms on

earth but not only is this my first time being an animal but the first time being a cat! I chose being a cat because I knew I'd have protection with my teeth and claws if needed. The other reason I chose to be a cat is because I knew that my mum only wanted cats in her life.

"My Dad needs to develop patience because that's his growing edge. I know I try his patience a lot. Sometimes he's very patient with me and other times he gets really frustrated. I'd say in the ten years I've been with him, his patience has grown slowly, and I've learned a lot about human's boundaries from him.

"For instance, humans don't like it when I attack their ankles with my claws out in order to get their attention. They also don't like it when I grab food off their plates when they're not looking. I'm also learning to trust humans. I'm learning how to be more affectionate as my trust grows. I'm cuddling up to my mum more, whereas before I'd sit away from her. The more I surrender to trust, the cuddlier I become.

"I've been with my family for ten years, and it's taken me this long to snuggle up beside them when we're watching TV. I chose you (Karen) because I knew you'd help me make the decision as to whether I leave my body or to stay in it when I was so sickly at only ten weeks old. It was my first time learning to trust a human being and it was you. I needed you to help me to decide whether I really wanted to be a cat in this lifetime.

"The time, attention, energy, concern, and love you had for me (during the) three times you didn't think

I would make it I decided to stay in my body. I knew you'd take care of me should anything go wrong in my lifetime. That's what I needed to learn from you—trust.

"I help you, Mum, by bringing joy and laughter into your life. You take life really seriously, and you need to laugh and play more. I'm here to teach you to be childlike, to dance and sing. I love watching you be goofy. I act goofy with you because it brings you joy. Why do you think I love playing 'blanket monster' so much? Because it brings you joy. I also make you laugh with my 'cutie-pie' faces, do I not? You're also learning boundaries yourself, Mum. I know you want to hold us, pat us, cuddle with us alllllll the time, but it becomes suffocating, uncomfortable, and overstimulating.

"Over the last ten years, you've learned my boundaries and learned not to override them but to respect them. Why do you think I've had to bite you so hard? It's my way to tell you that it's too much and to back off. I know I hurt you, but that's what it takes for you to listen sometimes. You're much better at respecting my boundaries and you're now experiencing me coming to you for more cuddles because of it."

True story: It took writing this book for me to find out why Tenderfoot bites me so hard, but hearing what she shares, she's absolutely right. It's been a hard lesson for me to give her space, to not pat or scratch her all the time, to not force myself on her, but because I've backed off, it allows the space for her to come to me and curl up beside me.

This is a really great example of how we can learn from our animal friends and apply it to other areas in our life if we just allow ourselves to have an open mind and to think that we can communicate with them and tune into their preferences, their wants and desires.

Soul contracts: Choosing compromised bodies

Earlier in this book, Beamer was introduced, explaining that he had neurological difficulties as well as deafness and blindness. I asked Beamer to explain why he chose such a severely compromised body. He explained that when he was a human in his previous life, he had an older brother who was severely disabled and lived his life in a wheelchair. Beamer admitted he was very cruel and mean to his brother because he believed he (Beamer) was forgotten and neglected by his parents, so he took his anger, hurt, and frustration out on his brother. He said that to make amends for treating his brother so horribly, and to learn more about being disabled, he chose to be a deaf and blind cat with severe neurological issues. He said he needed to learn about compassion, trust, and unconditional love, and he believed this body was the only way he could learn those lessons.

After three years of working with Beamer to make him comfortable, he told his mum, Jen, and me, that he was done. He told us that he learned all he needed and that he was now unnecessarily suffering. He needed to be released from his body. He couldn't handle it anymore. The rescue, Vancouver Orphan Kitten Rescue, (VOKRA), Jen, and I all agreed it was the most humane thing to do for him. I talked with him at the time of this writing, asking him if we made the right decision to help him die. This was his response:

"My experience of dying was great! I was surrounded by the people I love and who loved me. You guys made the best decision for me. I was miserable at the very end of my life. I know I was a young cat when I died, but the disabilities I had were overwhelming, and it was so hard to exist in that body. I learned lessons in the years I was alive, and I made amends. I did what was set out to do in that physical body. I have a deeper under-standing of compassion and trusting others to take care of me. I had to fully surrender to their care; I had no other choice. Above all, I have empathy for others who are compromised. I couldn't keep existing in that body; it was malfunctioning, and it was time for me to go.

"I'm going to stay where I am for now [in the rainbow pasture]; I'm not interested in becoming a human again just yet. I tried it, but I didn't like it. I think I have more to learn before I transition to the human species. I'm still in the rainbow pasture enjoying my existence here. I'm learning lots from other species. I'm taking my time deciding if I want to be a rabbit; they're pretty interesting creatures, or an elephant, or maybe if I want to come back as a cat. I still have to experience what it's like being in a healthy cat's body. I don't have to decide until I'm good and ready, and there are so many species to choose from. I think about being an elephant because of the bond that they have with one another, especially

the females. I think I'd like to experience that kind of a family dynamic first before being a human again.

"So, yes, everyone made the right decision to help me leave my body. I guided Jen to help release me from my body especially when she was sleeping. That's when I would be able to talk with her the best because her mind was open and more receptive to my messages. It was the life I needed to learn and make amends and I'm glad I went through it, but I'm also glad I'm no longer in that body."

Regarding an animal choosing the lesson to learn or the body to inhabit, an animal's soul can also choose to not continue living in their physical form after birth. While writing this book, I had the experience of working with a client's German Shepherd, Dove, who was pregnant and gave birth to one stillborn, "Sleeping Beauty," and one who survived the first 36 hours, "Peanut". I had the unique experience and opportunity to work with Dove, Sleeping Beauty, Peanut, and five other thriving and healthy puppies just a few hours after their birth.

I was able to see into Sleeping Beauty's body; she had an underdeveloped heart that could not pump enough blood through the size of a newborn puppy. Sleeping Beauty explained that her soul chose not to inhabit the body knowing the body's heart was too small.

As for Peanut, she was on a very fine line between life and death. It could've easily gone one way or another. She was failing to thrive regardless of the multiple tube feedings, stimulation, warmth from her puppy siblings and heating pad, tons of love, and the energy work I supported her body with. After the struggle of keeping her body going, Peanut's soul decided not to continue in a compromised body. Peanut's soul said she had a purpose and had goals she wanted to achieve. However, the compromised body was going to get in the way of both herself and the people who would become her family. She decided she would reincarnate to another litter at some point in the near future.

Again, it was a comfort for my client to know that she had done nothing wrong. Sometimes it's just the animals' soul's choice—in this case, to not continue in the compromised body she was assigned for one reason or another. I'm sharing this because I realize how important it is for us humans to know that sometimes our animals' deaths have absolutely nothing to do with our choices or actions—sometimes, it's just the will of their soul. We'll discuss more on this in the chapter on euthanasia and comfort measures.

Transitioning

I've helped countless animals leave their bodies and cross over the rainbow bridge. I've seen the bridge; I've seen the land they get to enjoy while they're in spirit form. The animals aren't afraid of death; they understand the death and dying experience. For them, it's just another process of life and not the end; it's just another step in their soul's evolution.

As I was writing this book, I had an incredibly rare experience happen with a client's cat, Luna. I usually get clients calling before their animal friend dies or afterwards but never during the death of their fur-kid. Luna was in a serious accident that severed her lower spine, and while trying to escape from the incident, she ran up a tree but then immediately fell out of the tree because she lost the sense of feeling in her legs and she lost her balance. My client immediately Face Timed me. In that moment, I placed my etheric hands into her energy field to help facilitate an easy transition out of her body. (My client and I both realized there was no saving this girl.) I felt her life force begin to fade away in my hands while I said the Crossing Over Prayer. As soon as I no longer felt her life force in my hands, I immediately saw four angels appear on all sides of Luna's soul, protecting her as they went over the Rainbow Bridge and into the Rainbow Pasture. It was at this moment that I really and truly understood that Luna didn't die; she literally just stepped out of her "fur coat".

When I'm in an end-of-life communication session, it's usually the animals who are comforting their humans to let them know they're not going anywhere. A lot of the time they're a bit confused as to why their humans are crying because for them it's just another stage of life. Without fail, at some point, the animals will explain to their humans they are literally just taking off their coat but who they are in essence doesn't stop living; they're just in another form of energy, just like how water can turn into steam. It's still there, but it's not as easy to see.

The biggest message that animals wish their humans to understand is that when they are in the process of transitioning from the physical form to energy, they're not going anywhere—not until their humans are ready or when they've been called to do a job. (Yes, animals have jobs in their non-physical form, but we'll get to that later.) I want to pause a moment to address humans not being ready because this is something our animals feel deeply. Here's an example:

Shortly before writing this book, I had a client whose dog, Max, was near to transitioning but was holding on until his human could get used to the idea of Max not being around for much longer. Even though my client told Max he would be okay and to just let him know if it was his time and he needed assistance in dying, Max said, despite his human's words, he sensed they weren't congruent with his human's inner energy about "losing" him. Max waited an extra week before he chose to leave his body.

At the time of writing this, I asked Max how he knew when his dad was ready to say goodbye to him. This is what he had to say:

> *"It took a week for my dad to come to terms that I was ready to exit my body. I could feel his emotions; he was getting used to the idea of not having my physical body in his life anymore. It wasn't until he said he was ready, it was time to let me go, and that he would be okay that I truly knew it was okay. It was incredibly helpful that he told me he was going to be okay. It was helpful to hear him say those words that he was ready because then I knew I could leave my body with confidence that he was prepared and was in fact ready for a life without my physical presence."*

I asked Max if it's important that his dad continues to talk with him as if Max were physically present. This was his response:

> *"It's about comfort for him. I want to know what's going on in his daily life. It's comforting to humans to know that we can still hear them and see them. As for me, I like hearing his voice and I love that he talks*

to me. I just wish he knew this beyond a shadow of a doubt. It's hard to watch your human in pain after we've left our bodies. If they could only see, hear, and feel us at this higher vibration of energy, because we are in fact still here. We haven't gone anywhere. Remember, Karen, I told him through you, that he needed to continue to talk out loud to me because I'm still going to be around him and in his life checking in on him from time to time."

Animals can't stress enough how they want their humans to continue talking with them and confiding in them like they used to. They want their humans to take a quiet moment each day to connect with them by picturing them in their person's mind's eye and having a conversation with them and then "seeing" how their animal would normally respond by purring, wagging their tail, licking them, or some other action. This is a form of animal communication that a lot of people don't acknowledge, understand, or recognize as such. The animals can't stress enough how important it is to them their person continues to interact with them as they believe it will also help them to heal a lot faster versus believing they're permanently gone and that's it.

A lot of the time, however, I have to explain to the animals that human eyes can't see the animals in spirit form, and they only see the physical form because we live in a physically dense state of being; our eyes don't have the ability to see higher levels of frequency, unlike animals, who can see spirits with their physical eyes. I must explain to them that humans believe that once the physical bodies are gone, we tend to believe that that is it—the animal no longer exists.

This is a concept most animals have a hard time comprehending because it's almost impossible for them to grasp the idea that life is finished once the physical body is no longer in motion. This is where confusion lies for the animals when they feel and see their humans' grief, yet the animals know their energy isn't going anywhere. They wonder why their humans can't understand that.

My girlfriend, Janine, adopted Digby back in 2003 when we were in graduate school together, so I have known Digby since she was a puppy. Digby and I spent a lot of time together over the years; I considered her my canine niece and we had an undeniable connection. We loved each other unconditionally and loved spending time together every chance we got. When it was Digby's time to leave her body, I got the fateful call from Janine asking me if I could come to the vet hospital to do a final communication session with Digby, her, and her husband, Darryl, Digby's human "parents". Digby and I had a lovely, intimate time sharing our favorite memories and times together and how impactful Digby was in our lives, all while giving gratitude to Digby for being such an amazing companion for those years.

Closer to the time that we needed to say our goodbyes was when I heard it for the first time: "Why are you crying? I don't understand." The three of us looked at each other surprised and perplexed because it was obvious, to us, why we were crying. We asked her why she was having a difficult time understanding this? She then said, "I'm just taking off my jacket; I'm not going anywhere." We explained to her that, as humans, we won't be able to physically touch or see her anymore or have the physical experiences of play fighting, walking in the forest, and snuggling. She thought it was the oddest concept that we were grieving over her. She then asked, "Do you cry when you take your jacket off?" We laughed while answering her "no." She then said, "Listen for me, talk with me and feel my answers in your heart because I won't be going anywhere. I haven't stopped existing."

I said my final goodbyes to this precious girl and left Digby and her parents to have a final few moments on their own. Time and time again since that moment, I've heard countless animals saying the exact same thing to their humans when they're about to transition from the physical form to the spiritual form of energy.

The bottom line: Just because we can't see or touch our animals physically, doesn't mean they stop existing or aren't showing up in our lives. They can't stress that enough. The loss we experience at not being able to touch their fur, or laugh at their play, or walk with them in the woods is real and deeply felt, but their continued existence as spirit and energy is also real and can be tapped into. The animals recommend we sit quietly every day and talk with them and see what comes up in our hearts because that is how they are trying to communicate with us from the beyond.

Knowing when it's time

One of the biggest questions I get asked is "How do I know when my animal is ready to leave their body?" It's one of the hardest decisions a person can make for their animal. Most people feel such a heavy sense of responsibility for their animal's life, and they don't want to make the wrong decision for them. No one can ever explain the level of pain we experience when having to make this decision. Yes, we are guided by our veterinarians and specialists through what needs to happen, but ultimately, the decision lies with us to make. We don't want to let them go too soon when they have a little spunk left in them or too late when they're suffering or in pain. It's such a fine balance, and we always want to do what's best for our animal.

So, how do you know when it's the right time to say goodbye to your beloved companion? That's where I come in. I always ask that question to their animal friend and let them make the decision. They're the ones who know best whether or not they are ready to leave. Sometimes they just need a couple more days, sometimes they hang around for a few more weeks to make sure their human(s) will be emotionally ready, and sometimes they need to be released from their body as soon as possible.

I ask if they're in pain, if they're suffering, if they're ready to leave their body, if they need and/or want to stay in their body a while longer. If they've said they're not quite ready to leave, the next step is to figure out a way for them to communicate with their human when it is time. I then ask both my client and the animal if there is a place in the house where their fur kid hates to go to, that they'd never ever go to for whatever the reason may be. My client will give me a room or a place in the house where their animal normally won't go into; their animal will concur and then an agreement is made for when they need to tell their person that it's time for them to leave their body. Nine out of ten times, the animal will go to that place in the house and their person is always shocked.

This exact scenario happened to me twelve years ago, before I had a much larger understanding about dying and death. I asked my senior rabbit, Pepper, (who, at thirteen years old, lived in a sixteen-square-foot area in our kitchen) how I would know when it was time for her to leave her body.

She said, "I'll be on my back."

I replied, "What do you mean you'll be on your back? How are you going to do that?"

She repeated, "I'll be on my back."

The next morning, I found her on her back, and I was gutted. I didn't want to acknowledge it. I wasn't ready for her to leave even though I knew her body was failing her. I unfortunately put my needs ahead of hers because I was in denial, so I just ignored that she was on her back.

That night, she was on her back again and my husband told me, "Karen, she's on her back again and she told you she'd be on her back when it's time for her to go."

So, the next morning I made the appointment to go into the veterinarian's to say goodbye.

Another example is when my sister Ainsley's dog, Kaia, had late-stage cancer and we knew at some point she would need to be released from her body. I asked Ainsley where the one place in the house was that Kaia never, ever went. She said it was downstairs into the basement. "She hates going down the stairs and never goes down," Ainsley said. We asked Kaia to go down the stairs to let Ainsley know when she was ready to be released from her body. The next morning, Ainsley got up and couldn't find Kaia. Her heart dropped, realizing that Kaia might be downstairs. Sure enough, Kaia was at the bottom of the stairs in the basement. Ainsley said that she couldn't bring herself to acknowledge that Kaia was ready to leave her body, that it was so soon for her, and she didn't want to say goodbye; she was heartbroken. The next morning, again, Ainsley woke up and went looking for Kaia, but this time she went straight downstairs and there Kaia was, at the bottom of the stairs in the basement. Ainsley immediately made the call to the vet to come over so she could leave her body.

Dear Reader, when you know the time is near for your beloved animal friend to leave their body, you can directly ask if they can give you sign or a signal. You can do this by closing your eyes, moving your mind's eye down to your heart, feeling the love you have for your animal friend, and saying the following to them:

> "Dearest [Spot/Fluffy/Cutie Pie….et cetera], I see that you're struggling and in pain. I only want the highest good for you and to do what is needed. I'm asking for you to tell me when you're ready to transition out of your physical body and I will help facilitate that for you. I know that you absolutely hate going to the basement, bathroom, guest bedroom, kitchen etc… so please go to that part of the house so I know for sure what I need to do for you to help you transition."

Take your time in saying this. Make sure it's heartfelt, mindful, and connected in love with your animal. Once you've finished, picture in your mind's eye that area of the house and "take a snapshot" of it and "send" it to your beloved friend. They will understand, so don't be shocked when you find them in that part of the house one day. Be gentle with yourself if you go into denial or if you doubt yourself when you see this, as it's an especially difficult time to acknowledge that your animal friend is ready to leave the physical body.

To recap the finer points of wisdom this chapter offers, I'm going to allow Trick to explain his philosophy on physical death:

"*When an animal dies, it's expected that the animal is gone (from the human's perspective), that it doesn't exist anymore, that's it, life is gone, nothing exists after the physical body dies. What the humans' eyes fail to see is the actual lifting out of the soul of the body; the body is the housing of the soul. If human eyes could see the soul rising out of the body, then humans would have a much deeper understanding of what it means to die and for the soul to live (on).*

"*If humans could see the soul lifting out of the body, then there would be a greater understanding, however, human eyes aren't meant to see the frequency of the animals' souls, or souls of any living being. That's the veil that's been put on humanity, not being able to see, feel, touch, smell the essence of the soul. Humans have come down to this physical realm to experience whatever it is they want to experience or need to experience in order for their souls to grow and expand, but in order to come down to the physical realm, part of being in human form is the forgetting part, the part where humans forget that they're all connected and one.*

"*We, as a herd of horses, animals, and lifeforce, inherently know that we're all one and we don't forget this; it's with us all the time. Why do you think the herds will react to predators all at once, or to stormy weather when we turn on a dime all together or like the starlings in a murmuration? We have a hive mind knowing we are all together; we haven't forgotten. Whereas the humans have forgotten, but that is the deal—you're human and you are required to forget the oneness and connectedness of humanity. It's the soul's task to remember the oneness of all living life force that swirls in, out, and around everything on the earth plane. So, humans believe that once the physical body dies that's the end of life which is the falsehood, that's the joke of it all—all that fear is for nothing. All that worry of the unknown is for nothing, all that concern, fear, worry, about physically dying and all of a sudden everything going black and that's it, it's all for nothing.*

"If humans only knew instinctively that when our physical bodies die that's not the end of our lives, that's just the beginning. People would live their lives in such amazing ways and fully and truly be in awe of the magnificence of being alive in the physical body and never take it for granted. What animals want their humans to know is that there is absolutely nothing to fear or be sad about when your animal dies. The only thing that is different is that your animal's body doesn't move anymore, that's it. We've just shifted into another vibration and frequency; we can hear and see you and talk with you but… it's hard to watch my humans be in so much pain crying, yearning, wanting me to be back in the physical body so they can touch me and see me. I'm still there with them. Nothing, and I mean nothing, has changed. It saddens me to know they're in pain and I can't do anything about it. Human ears aren't built to hear well, human eyes aren't meant to see well, and yet, we're there but we've just shifted to a different frequency.

"The best analogy I can give you is that you're listening to the FM radio station, and you decide you want to

hear the traffic report on the AM station (you tune into the traffic report knowing the FM radio station is still there, you've just changed channels and can no longer hear it). This is the same for when we leave our bodies; we've just changed frequency, but we don't stop existing. You just can't hear us. We're asking you to trust us as you trust the radio stations will still be there when you tune back into them. Trust us that we're still with you and haven't gone anywhere and will only leave once we're called to do so by a higher calling of our spirit and soul."

CHAPTER 8

EUTHANASIA, COMFORT MEASURES, PAIN, AND SUFFERING

I wanted to know how animals felt when their humans couldn't afford to pay for life-saving surgeries, comfort measures, or euthanasia. Having to make the choice to implement any of these things is a dilemma that many people around the world face every day. These are our animals that give us comfort, fill our lives with joy and humor, and are always there for us. They are beloved members of our family, but when illness strikes or an accident happens and we can't afford the surgeries or treatments to save their lives, it can be devastating for us.

Most people really want to know if their animals are in any pain and, if so, to what degree? Is there anything they can do for them to make life a bit more comfortable? People want to know if their animal is getting enough food or is hungry, how they can make eating food easier, and are they ready to pass on and leave their body? They want to know how they will know it's time to help their animal companion transition out of the body. They want to know what course of treatment they would like to follow or if there are different options. How can they show their animals how much they love them? Usually, there is a sense of urgency to make sure the animal knows they're not alone and they're deeply loved. And they want to know if their animals have any preferences that will help them to make the last few days, weeks, or months easier on them?

It never ceases to amaze me the diverse number of answers their animals have for these common questions. Comfort for one animal may be to simply be right up against their human, always with them, never to be left alone. However, on the other side of the spectrum, it could be to just leave them alone but to still be where the action is around the family activities, so they feel connected.

What you choose to do for your animal, especially if you haven't used an animal communicator to understand their preferences, may be a matter of what you've been taught to believe about life, death, and the medical interventions that land in between. Given my line of work, my purpose and calling, I'm obviously a proponent of asking your animal and taking their lead. Only they can inform you of whether they are in any pain, if they feel they are suffering, if they'd like to try a medical intervention, or if they're ready to shed their coat. Still, I must acknowledge the religious and spiritual beliefs that exist regarding the ending of life and how that can influence a human's decision about what to do for their animals.

There are many religions that believe it is wrong to euthanize animals; they believe euthanizing your animal, instead of letting them die naturally, is immoral, for it separates the animal's soul from its life path and/or karma. For those of us who see this as cruel and inhumane, we may need to examine our own judgments and biases towards death and those of different religions and belief systems.

Many of us believe it is cruel and inhumane when the animal is suffering and in pain to not euthanize our animal. Is this because we cannot handle our own personal human suffering therefore, we anthropomorphize our animals? Is it because we as a culture consider death as taboo and we can't talk about it rather than embracing it as part of the cycle of life? We can't avoid it, we all die, everything that is living dies—so why not embrace it and see it as a part of our existence versus something that we do our best to avoid, not talk about, or not think about?

As such, it's important we better understand how animals feel about all of this. We apply our human consciousness to these decisions, but our animals, as you now realize, have a very different perspective as sentient beings, especially those who choose their dying circumstances. As an animal communicator, my job is to provide a telephone line between the animal and their person while being as close to 100% accurate as possible; this is highly important when it comes to a session to determine whether the animal wants to leave their body via euthanasia, stay in their body a little longer (and then euthanize), or die naturally. In this chapter, I share what I've learned in speaking with spirit and animals who have experienced the difficult decisions their humans have had to make on their behalf.

In communing with spirit, I've learned that animals don't understand the concept of money; they just know they're hurting and in pain. Without that concept of money, the thing they trust is that their humans will make the best decision they can for their (the animal's) highest good and well-being. Animals also have an innate understanding that when they leave their body—however that death comes about— it signals it was their time to transition out of their physical form.

Because animals choose when and how they're going to die and who they'll be surrounded by, humans must understand that their money and finances don't dictate how their animals are going to die or transition. The human's lesson in this is to make the right decision for the highest good of everyone involved, including their animal. Humans are the ones who create meaning and determine what is valuable to spend their money on. But spirit knows that all life—whether human or animal or some other living creature—is valuable and there is no monetary amount that can be measured. Specifically, Spirit said:

> *"Money doesn't have a lifeform from which it needs to breathe. It is just a piece of paper that has printed ink on it that assigns a [numerical] value to it that humans make a meaning out of. When an animal passes and/ or transitions out of the body (via euthanasia) because the humans don't have (the) money (for life saving surgeries) it doesn't mean anything to their animals; all it means is that the animals aren't suffering anymore, and that's what they need—to be out of their pain-body. They understand that their humans are doing their very best at all times; (they do) what they can for them. They trust their humans to always make the best choice for their well-being; money is of no use or value to the animals. They trust that if they are meant to leave their body, then that was what was planned prior to them coming into the physical form of a horse, dog, cat, bird, reptile, or sea creature."*

Simply put, animals do not have judgments or beliefs about whether their humans should pay for life-saving measures. All they need to know is they are loved and supported through their transition process in whatever form that takes. Whether treatments or life-saving measures are available or not, there are still lessons for the soul to learn within the experience of death and transition, however it comes about. There is a much greater plan and path no matter how animals shed their fur.

Humans would be better off in understanding all of this. It would save them the grief, guilt, and embarrassment that goes along with making a hard decision of euthanizing their animals because they don't have the money to help them or choose not to spend their money in that way. Being able to communicate with your animal about their preferences can support a human (or family's) decision and ease the burden of deciding. Let me tell you the story of Blaze.

For a few years, I worked closely with an aging, beautiful, sweet-natured border collie, Blaze. The focus of our time together was to make sure he wasn't in any unnecessary pain, to communicate with his mum what he'd like to have happen on his walks, and to identify what kind of daily support he needed. When Blaze was no longer able to get up off the floor or he needed help walking to get his food, his human, Petra, and I knew it was time to have a conversation with Blaze about if, how, and when he'd like assistance in leaving his body. Specifically, we asked Blaze what his thoughts were on choosing to die naturally or be euthanized. This was Blaze's answer:

"I think I would want assisted death. There is no point to live in a body that isn't functioning; it causes too much pain for the humans, and a lot of suffering in the animal's body. The soul is its own entity within the body

of an animal. The physical body is just the container of the soul to experience life on the physical plane."

We asked Blaze about whether the soul suffers while the physical body is in pain. He shared that the soul feels the effects of the physical body because they are attached, but the soul doesn't suffer to the same degree. He also informed us he knew exactly when and where he would die, but that it didn't serve his human to know this. Specifically, he said:

"She has her own path to go through experiencing her animal, me, going through physical pain. She has her own ideas, belief systems, and values around death and as she's experiencing and witnessing the breakdown of my body, it's for her to come to terms, getting her ready for a life without me in it. The gift of a body that is breaking down allows the human to start expecting a life without their beloved animal in it. It's like a time period of preparing for that eventual loss."

Blaze also understood that humans don't see this period as a gift but as a significant stressor. They resist the eventual loss of their animal. He said:

"They take on their animal's pain as if it is their own. I know it is hard for humans to separate themselves from their animals' pain, yet I implore them to so they can spend every present moment experiencing their beloved animal, being with them, comforting them, versus spending their time with all the busyness of

appointments, setting up tests, exams, [and] protocols of treatments."

When I asked Blaze if he's saying humans shouldn't go through all the vet's suggested protocols to take care of their animals, he replied:

"I'm not saying stop doing what you must do to help your animal; I'm saying put it into perspective. Put it on the side where it belongs and do not get consumed by it. Spend time being with your animal, comforting him/ her, sharing your favorite experiences with them. We hear you, we feel your love, we understand what you're saying. You're comforting us. That love frequency helps us in ways that humans don't fully comprehend yet.

"The frequency of love resonates at such a level that it is the bond that connects all aspects of life forms together. What I mean [is] that love is the thread that weaves itself through all. It's the essence in the physical bodies, the soul as you call it, is what is important because it's everlasting. The physical body doesn't last, it [will] eventually have to break down to set the soul free. That will happen only when the lessons that soul has set out to learn have been reached."

I inquired about Blaze and his soul's lessons. Had his soul learned what it set out to? He believed it had:

"I've learned about unconditional love; I've learned that humans can be wonderful, kind, caring, loving.

I've also learned that humans are a very complicated species. My soul wanted to experience a family situation to be able to serve the humans by giving them joy in my antics, showing them they need to spend more time in the present moment and appreciate what's in front of them. I did this by smelling the flowers, by sniffing the grass, by jumping around and showing them [with my] joy. I am hoping that this frequency of joy will influence their emotional well-being."

At the time Blaze and I had his conversation, he wasn't quite ready to leave his body. Even though he knew he couldn't hear or see very well, and he had some pain, he still believed he was serving his humans by teaching them how to care for the frail, how to have patience, understanding, compassion, and empathy. Blaze believed this was mostly for the children in his family. His mum already had a deep understanding of these qualities.

"I want my human sister and brother, who are young, to understand the cycle of life. They've got the playing and being silly with [me]down pat. It's the part of my body that is frail that I want them to learn about how to take care of me, to have patience, to love no matter what the physical body is showing and/or demonstrating. I'm hoping that, in turn, they'll be able to take care of their parents when they're old and need support. I'm letting them practice with me first."

Each one of us who has animals in our lives that we cherish and adore is doing the very best we can at all times. We are doing the best we can given our beliefs or our culture or our bank account, meaning, the decisions we make at our pet's end-of-physical-life transition are the best we can do in that moment in time, given their or our circumstances. Our animals aren't holding any judgment, anger, or resentment towards us when we choose not to use comfort measures or we choose euthanasia. They know well before we do how they will die, and they understand that within those circumstances is a piece to their soul's expansion even if it physically doesn't feel good. They understand the physical discomfort is temporary. They understand their humans are loving and caring for them in the best possible way they can. When we can make peace with these ideas, we can find serenity and can spend more of our time focused on the remaining precious moments with our animal's physical self before they move on.

CHAPTER 9

THE RAINBOW BRIDGE, AFTERLIFE, AND REINCARNATION

One particular cat, Dottie, passed away in November 2022 from a genetic kidney disease at two years old. When her mum asked if she would visit her and be near her, Dottie showed me an image of the rainbow bridge, the river that flows under it, and the pasture beyond. Dottie then showed me how she will dip her paws into a portal that appears in the river and be able to "come home" and be with her mum and other cat siblings. I had never seen this image before. When I asked for clarification, she said the river can be used to go back to visit their humans or can be used as a looking glass to keep an eye on their families while staying in the pasture beyond.

One cat, Panda, told me that as much as she likes to revisit her family—which she's been doing on and off for the last decade—she now has a purpose, a job to do in patrolling the perimeter of the rainbow pasture. She's now become security on the "paw patrol" and she takes a lot of pride making sure all residents in the rainbow pasture remain safe and happy. When I asked her why the rainbow pasture needed to be safe and protected, she said there are nefarious energies that would do anything to gain access to the pasture and its residents. (Side note: dark or nefarious entities prey on humans' and animals' souls, as they are prized "commodities" and a source of energy/food to keep them existing.)

Every time I work with animals who have passed over, they show me an ever-expanding and infinite space of rolling hills, wildflowers, butterflies, and lots of sunshine; the sun is always shining. There are all types of species, except humans, living harmoniously in the rainbow pasture. There's a river that meanders through the pastures and oftentimes the animals—predators and prey alike—are playing with and chasing each other. There are cats chasing butterflies and small birds, there are bunnies that chase each other, horses that are enjoying their herds and reuniting with family members old and new. There's wildlife and domestic animals living in peace and enjoying one another.

The impression I get from the animals is that this place is a resting place where their souls can rejuvenate and until they're ready to come back to the earth plane to learn, grow, and serve. They can choose to stay however long they'd like, and they know that this pasture is "home" to them; it is their permanent residence.

Trick has shared with me what it's like. He says, "Once you cross the rainbow bridge, you go through a set of gates that automatically open for you. There's a river that runs under the bridge, but it connects to all the pasture lands. There is everything a horse, or animal, could ever want here. There's serenity, peace, a sense of knowing that no harm shall come to any of us. We all live in peace, respecting and loving one another as it should be on the earth realm."

When I asked him if the rainbow pasture is heaven for the animals, his response was, "It's more like a realm. It has heaven-like qualities of love, understanding, patience, respect, and love. Heaven is this realm for us. I don't know what it's like for people as humans don't live here. This is our sanctuary; it's our place to just be any animal we want to be. We need a break from humans—we need to just be without the limitations, expectations, and abuse of humans. There are many animals here who have been tortured, abused, and neglected by humans. They must rest as long as they need to in order to be able to go back to the earth realm if they so choose."

At the time I spoke of this with Trick, I asked him if he was still there or if he had chosen to go back down to the earth realm. His response included details that echoed what Dottie had once shared with me about the river. He said:

"I'm still here keeping an eye on my human, Hannah. I contact her through the looking glass in the river. The river itself is one big looking glass and a portal if you so choose to go through it to be near your humans in spirit. I'm not going to reincarnate until I know that my human is in better shape; it was a shock to her system when I left my body. Even though I knew it was my time to transition out of my body, I hoped I'd have more time on the earth realm. However, I also knew that Hannah needed me whenever she traveled, so I'm now able to be with her when she travels whereas before I was limited to the pasture four hours away from her. Now I can be with her, looking over her and watching out for her wherever she goes. I live in her heart and come to her in her dreams.

"*Whether or not she remembers is not important; it's a matter of the soul and spirit making connections with me that then sends the information to her subconscious. This is how it works for most animals connecting with their humans. When humans dream, they are not connected with their limited thinking (mind) that negates what they perceive to be impossible. When people are dreaming, it's easiest for us to visit our humans because there is no judging mind that gets in the way—it just is.*

"*I am currently with my original herd that my spirit/ soul was born into. They are my forever-herd, the ones that I know to be my family. When we're ready to reincarnate back to the earth realm, we say our goodbyes knowing that we'll come back together at some point. It would be the same for humans when they say goodbye to their families and go off to travel for weeks and months on end, but they come back to their families. It's the same for us; the rainbow pasture is our touch point to reconnect with our original herd. It's the same with all animals here. It's the place where we come back to, as it's our home and we know that we'll see our members at some point if we wait long enough before we reincarnate.*

"*The rainbow pasture, as you humans call it, is where our souls are born. It's a lovely 'landing spot' where our souls are created, and we are taught what to expect when we go to the earth realm. We don't immediately go to the earth realm once our souls are created. We learn from the other species; we learn what it's like to be all species, what their habits are, where they live, where they grow, what foods to eat, what to be cautious of, when it's dangerous and when it's safe to come out from hiding if we're prey animals, and when it's time to hunt when we're choosing to be predators. This is a place where it's safe for us to explore what it's like to be one species or another if we so choose. Some animals start as the smallest microbial and then decide to become an ant. Yes, we do have ants here—we have all the bugs and insects here. We learn from them as they learn from us. It's kind of like going from one classroom to another learning about one another, what you can expect when you choose that species and then are born into the physical realm called Earth. It's a fascinating process.*

"Overall, it's a place of learning, loving, respecting, educating, being educated, growing, expanding consciousness and awareness, and becoming sentient from an oversoul to individual souls even though we're all connected. I love the rainbow pasture; it's coming home from a very long journey to rest, to kick back and relax and reconnect with our soul family. When we're ready, we'll then go to the different species and begin to learn from one another to determine what we'll choose to be next or to decide if we want to stay in the same animal form as the last time."

Reincarnation

According to Trick, new souls can't just start off as a human being. They usually must go through different forms of life before they can even become an animal, let alone a human. Souls start out by being water, soil, grass, stones, plants, trees, overall nature. They need to experience being separated from the Divine Creator first before moving on to the next level of being an animal.

However, even within the animal kingdom there is a level of hierarchy and levels of consciousness that the soul needs to develop. Most living beings start off as bacteria, amoebas, or other forms of single-celled organisms. They then move on to being insects and then small creatures. They'll choose to develop into more complex animals with higher levels of consciousness. Once the soul develops into the highest level of consciousness such as whales, elephants, or horses for several lifetimes, they'll begin to learn what it means to be a human being in between lifetimes.

Animal form

As we discussed when talking about soul contracts, animals get to choose the physical animal life form they incarnate. The animal they choose to become can be for a variety of reasons, but it's all a part of developing the next level of their soul's expansion. And sometimes they might choose to come into their animal form to help with their human's expansion since their (animal) souls are tasked with helping humans in their souls' journey as well. An animal can also choose to reincarnate several times as the same type of animal.

One interesting interaction my colleague, mentor, and friend, Laura, told me she had was with a deer who was hunted for food. She's not a hunter herself; it happened on the property that she was visiting. The owner of the land needed help bringing the deer's body for processing. Laura recalled that when she went to help carry the body, the deer came to her and told her that he was happy to serve the family whose land he lived on and that this was the second time he had manifested into a deer to provide food for the family. He went on to tell Laura that the owner took really good care of the land, that he respected the land and the wildlife on it and maintained it well, caring for all life there, and that it was the buck's honor to have given his body to feed the family for that year.

This was the first time that both Laura and I heard about an animal choosing to reincarnate as an animal to purposefully give its life to feed a family as a way of thanking humans for taking such good care of the land. Since then, I've channelled the buck to better understand why he chose this specific reincarnation, not once but several times.

"The land that I chose to be raised on is not new to me. My soul has grazed in these fields for centuries. I have seen this land develop into what it is today. The man who takes care of the land has done a tremendous job not only in taking care of it but also in making sure that (the) wildlife is thriving. He has an innate understanding of how the ecological balance works. He uses his knowledge to ensure that the land is thriving for all living beings, including his family. There are very few people in the world who have this built-in understanding of how everything is connected. It is my way to give thanks to him and his family for taking such good care of all creatures who live off his land, of the land and the earth itself, and of his family.

I asked him to tell me about the day of the shooting. Why did he choose that day?

> *"I knew the man was thinking about hunting a buck that day; I could feel his energy. It changes when he gets into the mindset of hunting. His frequency and vibration changes. I don't think he's aware of it, but he does. I had been monitoring him and his energy frequency to determine what day he was going to go hunting. I was the right age, the right size. I was mature enough to be shot and given to the family. Once he got his energy frequency locked into his mindset that he was going hunting that day, I intentionally put myself in his line of sight, so he could have an easy shot. It's not a good feeling to be suffering in pain, so I knew I had to be in perfect view to make sure he had a clean shot so my body wouldn't suffer.*

> *"There was no fear because I decided to give my body to him. I know that the physical body isn't who I am; I am always connected to my Creator, to the One Source, who you call God. I know I am always living all the time; it's just a matter of whether I want to be in physical form or not. I will manifest into form again at some point. I'm not quite ready to go back; I have other things I need to do here in the rainbow pasture. I want to be with friends, family, to reacquaint myself with being back in spirit form and just rest. At some point when I'm willing to take the task up again to be in physical form, I will. I'll go back to that land, to be with that*

family and to give thanks again for the wonderful job that he and his family are doing, being good stewards of the land.

"There are many of us who come back to earth to give our physical life form over to humans as a way of thanks, of service. We choose those who have good and kind hearts and intentions, who don't waste the physical body, and who have an understanding of how precious life is. It's not something that is done for every hunter or farmer. It all has to do with how grateful the person is for all that they have.

"Please let your readers know that hunting has a place, it has a purpose as long as it is done for the right reasons, with a good heart and pure intentions, as long as they are grateful. I also want your readers to know that giving thanks for the meat they eat is important; it helps the soul of that animal to know that you appreciate their sacrifice. It is a sacrifice, and it can be painful if not done correctly. Whether or not you eat meat doesn't matter for most of us as long as you eat with gratitude, enjoyment, and an appreciation for the animals' sacrifice and service to the human body."

While the deer has reincarnated as a deer several times, eventually the deer's soul won't be able to grow and expand in that experience. They may have to reincarnate as a larger animal with a higher level of consciousness (such as the horse, whale, or elephant that Trick mentioned previously) or move on to reincarnate as a human when their soul is ready.

Human form

As mentioned at the beginning of this section, it's only once the soul develops into the highest level of consciousness, they'll begin to learn what it means to be a human being in between lifetimes. I asked Trick about the process by which animals might choose to become a human. This was his response:

> *"We choose to become human when our consciousness and experience can no longer grow and expand. We've hit a plateau and can't grow anymore. We decide at that point to remain as an animal and be of service to humanity or we choose to leave the rainbow pasture and learn from the angels who work with humanity to learn what it will be like to become a human leaving from an animal's body to a human body—what to expect, what you experience, what it will be like to have a voice, to be able to think independently and not be connected to a hive mind. They help us to understand it gets very lonely and upsetting for some first-time animal souls when they forget that we're all connected; the human mind is programmed to forget because this is the next level of expansion, learning, and growing. We have to become separated in order to grow and learn that in fact we're not separated and disconnected, that we're still all one together and connected to our Source, that place from which our souls were originally created."*

Some of us have heard of the rainbow bridge and may have believed this was an imaginative heaven for animals made up simply for the purposes of comfort rather than a real place. Yet, multiple animals have shared similar descriptions of the bridge and the pasture where their souls go to recharge, reunite, and eventually choose whether to reincarnate. From what I've seen via the images the animals have given me, it's a glorious and pure place. Personally, this gives me hope that if animals move on to such a wonderful light-and-love-filled place, something similar must await the souls of humans when it's our time. Regardless of what you believe about a human "heaven," rest assured your beloved animals are moving onto a beautiful resting place, a place where they're never far and always can look in on you whenever they wish and whenever you need them.

CHAPTER 10

GRIEF AND FAMILY LIFE AFTER AN ANIMAL'S PASSING

My cat, Curious, has polyneuropathy. She's not able to feel her feet, legs, and hips all that well. She needs acupuncture, chiropractic treatment, and laser treatments on a regular basis. The reason I'm telling you this is because there was a time when I couldn't get her into her regular sessions and had to wait another three weeks. By the time she was seen, she was six weeks overdue. She was stumbling, collapsing on her hind legs, and couldn't balance well when trying to jump to get onto my lap to sleep.

It was at this point that I really and truly recognized that she is not getting any better. In fact, the treatments are only keeping the degeneration of the nerves at bay. I had a sudden flash of panic go through my body with the realization that one day I, too, will be without my beautiful, ever-loving Curious. That thought struck me in my heart.

This is a cat who is a wise, old soul, and otherworldly. There is a depth in her that I can't quite put my finger on, but I've described her to people as a master teacher in cat form. I've had cats throughout my life, but this cat is something special. What I want to address is my own personal reaction and panic when I realized that one day Curious won't be in physical form— my heart was crushed. Here I am, writing a book on animals, their experiences and messages they want their humans to know about death and dying, and even though I understand rationally that the soul is the real essence and not the physical body, it really hasn't landed on me in the emotional level.

I definitely have my own fear of never being able to touch her exquisitely soft fur again, feel her purrs on my leg when she's falling asleep, or how she comforts me when I've been crying, how she hugs me by placing her head against my cheek, watching her zoom around the house, along with wobbles, falls, collapses, and play like a kitten when chasing a string across the floor. It's the comfort of knowing there is a sentient being in an animal form who is there to comfort me, to make me laugh, to bring joy into my heart when I've had a rough day at work. That's what I'll miss, and it's letting those experiences go once Curious leaves her body that I'll miss the most—the physical interaction with her. Yes, I'll be able to talk with her at any point in time knowing we'll always be connected, but that's different than being able to place a hand on her and feel the purrs underneath or the soft licks on my forehead that I'll miss.

We experience our animals—their soul, their humanity— as a part of ourselves. People tend to consider their animals as an extension of themselves. When an animal departs, it's not just a loss of a "thing," or of an object. It's the loss of the animal friend that cuts deeply to the heart, a piece of them gone forever. It's that illusion of the forever goodbye that creates the pain, longing, and deep loss that humans experience when our animal friends die.

Even while knowing all that you know now from reading this book, grief will still happen, the feeling of loss will still be there. I can't take that away for any of us, me included, no matter how much wisdom I have gleaned from animals. Grief is a part of the human experience. A lesson we are here to learn. My aim is to make it a little more tolerable, a little more hopeful.

To me, making it more tolerable and hopeful is rewriting the belief that nothing but what we see exists. That everything is final, everything else is finite, not expansive and continuing after we leave our physical bodies. This is when humans can really learn from their fur-companions by believing what they say about their continued existence after their physical body no longer exists; to understand that the Super Consciousness/Spirit/Universe/All That Is/God/Oneness is what keeps the energy of that animal and/or human going.

I want humans to understand their connections to their animals never breaks, never dies. It's always within our hearts. So, how can our connection to our animals continue after their physical body can no longer move, breathe, or animate?

That consciousness of the animal will continue living but in a different state of being, a different form of energy, and will continue to exist in our mind, heart, and soul. As time passes on, we may not think of them that often, however, the mere thought of them brings them back into existence and is as real as when they first came into our lives. Take away the façade of the physical bodies of humans and animals and we experience everlasting existence and consciousness, aware of one another always in a state of being.

Yes, it's acknowledged that we will miss the physical being of the animals, the physical warmth, their wagging of tails or purring voices, their cold little noses up against our cheeks, and their smooth or rough tongues licking our faces and/or hands. What we must remember is all we need to do is close our eyes, take some deep breaths, get connected into our hearts and out of our minds, and remember what our animals felt like when they were in physical bodies, and sure enough you will physically feel your animal as if they were right there. Immediately, memories of your shared experiences together become more prominent.

Who's to say that our animals no longer exist once they leave their bodies? We just have to practice connecting, remembering, feeling the love that you both shared together. THAT is the truth of existence, not the illusion of physical bodies. That physical pain of loss is what makes us human. It's what enriches our lives, to have experienced something so precious as having an animal companion enter our lives, our experiences, and our dreams.

The depth of loss can never be minimized just because it was a horse, cat, dog, bird, hamster, fish, reptile, etc. The ever-loving, unconditional acceptance our animal has for us enriches our lives always. We will carry that forward with memories. Our hearts have grown exponentially by having them in our lives; the memories will bring us back to those moments when they were in their physical bodies and remind us how to continue living with the growth we experienced. We'll never, ever be the same person ever again. They've enriched our lives so much that they've left an indelible mark, and we will always carry a footprint on our heart, mind, and soul.

Remember, those times when they've loved us when we're in emotional pain, physical pain, mental anguish—they continue to love us still, just from a different plane of being. They were our secret keepers and can still be if we trust they can hear us since they live in our hearts forever. They soothed us, they nurtured us with that unconditional love. Animals serve us in this way, to be our emotional support, mental support, and physical support. They help expand humanity's consciousness about animals and how smart, aware, and compassionate they are.

Do I or Do I Not Get Another Animal?

Another important question my clients ask is if they should get another animal after their beloved one has died. I can't answer that question for them, but what I can do is help facilitate a conversation with their animal in spirit to help them determine whether they're ready for another animal in their lives. Most of the time, the animals understand that their person is not trying to replace them but trying to fill a void in their lives after their animal's passing.

Animals in spirit serve their humans in numerous ways. Much of the time, their animal in spirit will tell them that they'll be sending another animal companion into their lives because their humans need to either expand their learning, be challenged in a particular area of development (such as me developing patience with my trickster of a cat, Tenderfoot), or perhaps the animal knows that their family is the perfect family for a rescue to come and take refuge with, to rest and heal. I've had animals tell their family members that their family's karma is to be of service to the animals that come into their lives by providing a loving, safe, healing household where they can just be, heal their spirit, and begin to trust humans again. I've had many times clients say to me they believe their previous animal companion sent the new animal to them because it challenges them in ways that only the first animal could know about.

Will My Animal in Spirit Come Back in Another Form?

Many of my clients want to know if their animal's spirit will come back to them in the form of another animal. This is a more complex question and sometimes the animals don't even know themselves because it all depends on what is the highest good for their soul's evolution. Some animals will say they will, but that's not the norm. In fact, they usually say they'll create an agreement with the new animal so that they'll be able to dip into the new animal's body and share the body for a while just to show their humans that they're still thinking of them.

For instance, my sister Ainsley's dog, Kaia, who passed away four years ago, used to walk in such a distinct way, crossing her back and front legs in front of each other, looking like she was walking on the diagonal, but she was able to walk straight. Ainsley's new dog, BlackJack, walks the exact same way at times, it's a specific, unique gait that is Kaia's "trademark". When I catch Jack walking this way, I instinctively know it's Kaia who's popped into Jack's body just to say, "Hi, I'm still here." The animals' spirit teaches the new animals all they need to know about their new family-the rules, the dos and don'ts, who is the discipliner and who is the nurturer.

For the animals who are left behind, one of their concerns is will their human be so distraught that they'll forget about them? This is a time when we must remember our other animals in the home who need more nurturing and attention than usual, other than regular walks, meals, and water. They'll want to be connected with you, assured by you that everything will be okay, while acknowledging this is the hardest time when we have to say goodbye to our beloved fur-friend. Remember, they're saying goodbye, too.

PART 4

The Lesson and the Invitation

CHAPTER 11

RE-EVALUATING WHAT WE KNOW ABOUT LIFE, DEATH, AND ANIMALS

I didn't get up one day with the idea to write this book. This book came to me directly from Source. I was told to give the animal's wisdom to the people. It's impossible to share everything I've learned from them, but the most succinct way to summarize their teachings is that they want us (humans) to learn from them a better way of living and dying. To re-evaluate what we think we know about our earthly, physical existence and the existential, spiritual one. So, before this book comes to a close in a few more pages, I'm offering additional wisdom and insight from the animals I've been honored to know and commune with, so you can live the most enriched, loving, and beautiful lives.

On love and kindness

Some of the most beautiful wisdom about love and kindness I've received has been from Hemi, whom you were introduced to earlier in this book.

"Love one another, be kind to one another. We live in a herd because we must depend on one another for safety, for companionship, for love, for growth, for wisdom. We pass our stories down from one generation to the next and each succession of generations holds the wisdom of the herd, what to eat, what to avoid, what people are good, have goodness in their hearts, which ones are evil, with bad intentions. We are wisdom keepers as are all species. Without this process we would be lost, there wouldn't be any guidance, no inner knowing of how life works."

Sunny, a bearded dragon, addresses the present moment saying, "It takes a special kind of mindset to have us as companions", meaning…

"Even though we don't show affection the way other creatures do, we show it in our own unique way. Just because we're cold-blooded animals doesn't mean we don't know how to feel love. Love is the energy that surrounds us all and you just have to tap into it to feel it from us. We show love by responding to you in our own way that for us is engaging, affectionate, kind, playful, and fun. We want to be connected to you; let us show you how."

On being present

After talking with hundreds and hundreds of animals over the years, the most common message that animals want people to know is to practice being in the present moment. Being in the present moment is where life exists. All there is, is now. It's this moment of being present when life happens.

Trick says, "To have a deeper relationship means being in the present moment with us." Trick explains his quote:

"We live in the present moment always. It's how we navigate through our experiences that make up our lives. We are more enriched when we smell every blade of grass, every flower, and feel the breeze in our manes. Being in the present moment allows us to appreciate life fully and deeply. Join us by quieting your minds and just be one with us."

Animals have a unique way of staying in the moment, perhaps because of how their souls are designed differently from ours. Humans seem to become more challenged with staying present the faster and more digital our world becomes. While animals don't have any consciousness perhaps of the digital world, they are attuned to our frequency, vibration, and energy and can tell when we are focused and fixated elsewhere. Curious does a great job pointing out how my husband and I are challenged with staying in the present moment:

"Humans, especially you, Mum, think too much in the future and worry about 'what ifs' instead of experiencing life right now, here, in this moment, and in this moment, and in this moment—see what I did there? Dad spends too much time in the past; his mind goes over and over the mistakes and choices he's made that he thinks were bad ones and regrets them. Again, it's

another way of missing out on what's happening in life, which is in this moment, right now. Why do you think I come snuggle with you and/or Dad? It's to help you to get present, to be with me. Why do you think I tap you on the arm when we're snuggling? It's because you're not paying attention to our present time together. I'm teaching you to come back to the here and now. Yes, I love the attention, but it's also to help you become more present and enjoy the moment."

I asked her what she'd suggest doing when humans are having a really bad day, and in the moment when we're feeling angry, hurt, upset, et cetera. She replied,

"Be with your feelings, but don't hold onto them. There's no point. If you hang onto your feelings, it just clouds over being in the present moment. It takes away from life happening. If you're feeling angry or upset, feel it but allow it to release, just like water going under a bridge or over rocks. It may be the same rocks the water is going over (symbolizes life) but the water is different, (symbolizing feelings), it passes. It's so much easier coping with life this way. What we as animals know is that life is not linear, it's always here in the now, just like the boulder in a river, always there, never moving."

But Curious isn't the only one with messages about being in the present moment. Rabbits like Pepper, and fish like Tony, have similar wisdom to impart about the power of being present.

Pepper puts a spin on the idea of presence by talking about having fun. "Just have fun, it'll make you younger."

> *"We may be timid but we're a lot of fun. Just get to know us and we'll surprise you what we can do. We may only hop around in your eyes, but we're creating fun for ourselves, to make you smile and laugh out loud. We're here to serve as the jokesters in your life. Play with us and you'll see what we mean."*

And Tony says fish can reduce your stress in the moment. "Watch us and your stresses will dissolve."

> *"We see the world in a different way than humans. We have more of a collective consciousness than individual minds. You see us inside something, we see humans outside of our environment that is foreign to us. You consider our tanks as keeping us captive but we're living our lives peacefully and aware. The tanks allow us to exist while we swim in our natural state of calm and peace. We sense how you humans have busy minds, thinking about everything else except for the present moment. Spend a few minutes a day consciously breathing while we swim. Use us to remind you of being present. We serve humans as a reminder to journey through life in a state of tranquility and peace."*

On being connected to nature

Knotts, Naomi's aunt's dog, offered his perspective of what it means to be "in the moment" and how people can reduce stress in their lives by being present. Specifically, Knotts wants humans to reconnect with nature. There is a universal oneness that we ALL belong to and can recognize and tap into when we take the time to notice the world around us and how we are all connected.

> *"If I had to choose one area to talk about it would have to do with walks. Walks are so important to the animals' minds. I mean, it stimulates us. How would you like to be in a house 24/7 without interacting with nature? We have to be out in nature because we ARE nature. We are an expression of nature, but people don't understand this at all. They don't see themselves as being part of nature and being connected with it. People think they know everything when, in fact, it's nature that knows everything. The earth tells me what I need to know about life: I can smell it; I can smell when [the] earth is fresh and alive with living organisms and then I can tell when the earth is dead and dry—I don't like that kind of earth. It saddens my heart.*
>
> *"People just go through their lives without stopping, breathing in the fresh air, without enjoying what rain feels like on your face, what snow feels like and being in the moment. There's not that much snow where I live, but when it happens, I love it! It feels so light, fluffy, and cool. I just love chasing the snowflakes. People just ignore all these incredible things that nature offers everyone to enjoy life, and it's free! You just have to be present in the moment. It fills up my heart. Why wouldn't it fill up people's?*

"I see so many people not tuned into nature and the oneness of it all. Instead, I sense that they're tuned out, talking on their phones, checked out as to what's really happening around them. Get off your phones, get off of your earphones, listen to the birds, they're singing you messages from the sky! Listen to the winds; they're whispering words of love from nature. Smell the fresh air; it literally gives you the oxygen you need to breath. Smell the fragrance of flowers; they're reminding your heart that we are all connected.

"The earth grounds us, keeps us centered, and the earth's energy that comes from it can heal us, but people have forgotten this. When you go outside, remember to be in the present moment and enjoy the gifts that mother nature is giving you every single day; it'll put a smile on your face, a pep in your walk, and joy in your heart. I see so many people disconnected, and it saddens my heart because they have no idea what it is that they're missing and how much joy it can bring to one's mind, spirit, and heart. Life is amazing and nature is the gift.

So, my message is for people, enjoy life through nature and be present; it's so wondrous, beautiful, and it's a part of who you are."

CHAPTER 12

YOU'RE BEING INVITED TO SPEAK WITH YOUR ANIMALS; WILL YOU ACCEPT?

Now that you have a new level of awareness and understanding of the beloved animal(s) in your life—their souls, their lives, their deaths—you can begin to cultivate a much deeper and richer relationship with them. This might be as simple as showing them more respect or paying closer attention to their behavior as a way of reading their signs and signals in effort to "hear" what they're trying to share with you. It might be by re-evaluating things such as their diet or why they always bark in certain scenarios. Perhaps it's in speaking with them out loud, now knowing they are listening, aware, and understand what you're saying. These are all beautiful first steps in taking what you've learned here and enriching your animal relationships.

There's another invitation that's open to you and that's to communicate directly with your animal via an animal communicator or telepath such as myself. I'm not the only one who exists by any means. Should you be curious, however, about working with me or someone else, I want to take the last few moments of this book to help you best prepare for this kind of exchange so you can get the most out of your experience.

During an initial consult, people tell me very briefly what's going on with their animal(s) and why they've contacted me. Sometimes they don't have specific reasons, they just want a wellness check to see how their animal is doing overall. Closer to the end of our conversation most people want to know how I talk with the animals, what they should do to get prepared for the session, and what they can expect. I explain to them, just as I've done in this book, how I become the animal'(s) voice.

The session will always be done on Zoom so that I can send a recording to them after the session for them to rewatch if they have any questions. I normally tell potential clients that all they need to do is make sure they have an updated version of Zoom available to them. However, the most important suggestion I tell clients is to have all their questions for their animals written down because thirty minutes will go by fast before you know it. With a list of questions ready at hand, you'll be able to keep yourself on track and get all your questions answered in the allotted time.

I tell my clients to imagine me as a telephone, and I'm just the translator from the animals' language to English. I don't remember the conversations I have with the animals; it's not for me to remember. (The stories told in this book were previously recorded in client sessions.) It's for the human and their animal companion to have an in-depth conversation about whatever needs to be discussed. During the conversation, I may ask questions in addition to my clients' to bring clarity to the answer given by their animal. However, about fifteen minutes after coming out of the zone, I don't remember at all what transpired between my client and their animal. I have a general idea, but not the details. I learned earlier in my career I need to record my sessions with clients because, without fail, my clients would ask me to remember what their animal told them about a certain topic, and I must tell them I don't remember. I send these recordings to the clients afterwards so they can refer to them when needed.

When you've booked a communication session with your animal, make sure you take time for yourself after the session, especially if it's regarding end-of-life care, planning, saying goodbye, etc. It's an emotional discussion to have with your beloved animal family member and you may not be up to going back to a work frame of mind. Instead, make sure you have at least an hour to yourself to cogitate and reflect on the conversation you've just had before you need to get back into the busy-ness of life.

Whether you book a session with an animal communicator right away, some time next week, or never, I hope you've found new perspectives to consider and a new way to see, understand, and be with your animals because of reading these pages. I intended to help you gain insight into your animals' needs, wants, preferences, and desires. I hope I've done so. I wanted you to be able to see your animals not as pets but as companions, as sentient beings who are compassionate, who serve us, and who are equal to us and not pets to own. I hope you now see them that way. I wanted you to develop a deeper connection with and gratitude for their presence in your lives. I hope that turns out to be true. And I hope beyond all hope to have offered you some peace of mind regarding your animal's journey in death.

Please take the insights shared here and spread the animals' wisdom and messages. Share this book with your animal-loving friends and family. Return to these pages again and again when you need guidance and comfort in your relationship with your animal whether they are physically here or not. The animals have guided me to give you this much, but they have more to offer you. Listen.

CROSSING OVER PRAYER FOR ANIMALS

The Crossing Over Prayer serves as a type of insurance policy that will ensure your animal's soul will be protected while crossing over into the Heavenly Realms of the Rainbow Bridge and Rainbow Pasture. This prayer can be said during your beloved animal companion's transition or after. If your animal is lost, hasn't returned home, and you believe your animal has died, reading this prayer out loud will ensure your animal's soul will be transported, protected, healed and returned to the Rainbow Bridge and Rainbow Pasture.

The Crossing Over Prayer

Almighty Divine Creator,

I respectfully request that you take into your loving arms (insert name)'s soul who has spent his/her lifetime serving me/us as a loyal and unconditionally loving animal companion so that [insert name]'s soul may go Home to the Heavens of the Rainbow Bridge and Rainbow Pasture, *right now.*

I pray with all my heart that my beloved animal, (insert name), receives the love, compassion and protection he/she needs as he/she journeys to and into the light and warmth of your Divine love, *right now.*

I request that your Angelic Team wrap (insert name)'s soul in your unconditional love for healing, soul restoration, and protection so that he/she may cross over into the Heavens of the Rainbow Bridge and Rainbow Pasture, *right now.*

I recognize and understand all animals' souls need and deserve to cross over to the Heavens of the Rainbow Bridge and Rainbow Pasture, acknowledging their significant contribution and service to humanity.

I hereby request that your Angelic Team cross over all animals' souls who were forgotten or unknown back over into the Heavens of the Rainbow Bridge and the Rainbow Pasture, *right now.*

Thank you, Divine Creator, for your assistance in helping me to help (insert name)'s soul and these lost souls to go home into your Heavenly Rainbow Pasture.

In gratitude, and so it is.

WAYS TO CELEBRATE YOUR ANIMAL'S LIFE AND SERVICE

Over the last decade, I've been amazed at the variety of ways my clients have honored their animals' lives after they've passed. These clients followed their hearts and created some amazing ways to honor and memorialize the life they shared with their beloved animals. I've included a list of some of my favorites below.

Personally, I'm not one to have a ceremony; I'm a pretty private person when it comes to grieving. My husband and I usually talk about our favorite memories and stories of our animals with one another. I've kept their ashes, kept snippets of their fur, and had their paws and noses imprinted in clay. I know their bodies aren't who my animals were, however, having a little something that's a physical keepsake I find is comforting to me, reminding me they are right there with me in spirit.

There is no proper way to celebrate or memorialize your animal's life. It's whatever you choose to do, or not do, that's the right way for you.

Here are some suggestions from my clients.

- Celebration of Life ceremonies with friends and family
- Hold a small gathering at the cremation sites
- Write a children's book in honor of your pet and hold a book launch at a local book and coffee shop
- Share stories about your favorite moments with your animal with immediate family members
- Make a picture album or design a photo blanket made with your animals' photos
- Keep a lock of their fur and/or whiskers with a favorite poem as a keepsake

ACKNOWLEDGMENTS

There are so many people I need to recognize who made it possible for me to finally get this book written. My family, first and foremost, have been unwavering in their support and encouragement. Drummond, my steadfast loving husband: you believed in me when I didn't believe in myself. You kept pushing me past my limits and kept doing it even when I resisted every step of the way. I love you deeply. Mum, Dad, Rona, and Ainsley—you have all been my main cheerleaders, believing in me, encouraging me to keep on trucking through the tough times and especially when I doubted myself and wanted to give up. You didn't give up on me and without your cheering me on, honestly, this book wouldn't have been written in the first place. My buster of a nephew, Nash, and my sunshine of a niece, Luca, my memories of you with your animals (so many foster kitties!!) past and present helped me when I had writing blocks. I thought about how they all loved you both so much and now their insights and wisdom are reflected in the written words. Thank you for keeping me laughing and keeping things real. I love you both so much. My awesome bonus-sons Fraser, Graham, and their beautiful wives, Meredith, Gilly, and of course my fun-loving granddaughters,

Willow, Elle, and Izzy, you provided me the space to laugh my head off, play, and be absolutely silly which was such a salve for my tired brain. You have no idea how much you helped me to decompress and just enjoy the moment!

I want to thank my two mentors and dear friends, Lynda Jane and Laura. Your willingness to take me on as your student has been impactful beyond words. You'll never know the degree to which passing on your knowledge and skills has made a difference in my clients' and their animals' lives, and for that, I'm deeply grateful.

Amy, you were the first person to help me with my mess of notes, got me on track, and cheered me on not only as an editor but also as a dear friend. Thank you from the bottom of my heart.

To my incredible editor, Ally. Right from the beginning, you took this project on with such gusto! I instantly knew when I received your enthusiastic intro video clip, you were exactly who I needed to make sense out of the mess of my thoughts and stories and turn it into an incredible manuscript. You honestly surpassed my expectations. You gently but firmly pushed me past my comfort zone and helped me to accomplish areas of writing I never thought I could. You made this reluctant writer an author! Thank you so very much.

Lisa, thank you for all your expertise in line editing; your knowledge and insight made the difference in turning this book from good to great. I'm so grateful for you!

To my visionary publisher, Susie, your coaching in the background, guiding me, cheering me on, and being excited for me kept me going with enthusiasm. I can hardly wait until we get to work together again. Thank you for your wisdom and expertise!

Carol Komitor of Healing Touch for Animals®, If it weren't for you, for your courses and your incredible support all those years ago, I wouldn't have been able to develop the deep passion and desire to help animals and their humans to the degree that I do.

I want to thank everyone who has ever booked a session with me and given me permission to talk with your animals. They were the ones who gently pushed me to write this book on their behalf.

I especially want to thank the following people and their animals because without you and them there wouldn't be a book. Your animals made it possible, and I promised them I'd create a platform from which humans will hear them. This is for you:

Naomi: Nacho, Hale, Knotts (dogs) Umbra, Persephone, Purrfect (cats), Codi & Hemi (horses), Einstein (bird). Thank you, Naomi, for such an incredible group of animals you connected me with!

Tanya: Rowley, Ziggy (cats), Jax and Jigs (dogs).... thank you, Tanya for being one of my very first clients and for a great office to work from. I'm so grateful for you!

Jen: Beamer (cat)
Ainsley: Blackjack, Kaia (dogs) and Honeybee (cat)
Nash: Sunny (bearded dragon)

Karen & Hannah: Gabby, Trick, and Sassy—Thank you for being my very first communication clients!

Janine and Darryl: Digby, thank you, sweet girl, for teaching me that we just take off our raincoats when we leave our physical bodies.

Majid and Scrunchy, I can't say enough of how much I deeply appreciate the two of you and your continued support.

Melodie: Poncho and Pippin
Petra: Blaze, Storm, Chase
Laura: Britta and Scoobie
Deirdre: Peanut & Butter
Tricia: Sophie

Special thanks to Karen and Maria at Vancouver Orphan Kitten Rescue Association for all their support over the years.

I'm so grateful for the following animals who agreed to contribute to this book: Celeste the horse, Dragon the dog, Magic the cat, Dove the dog, Luna the cat, Pepper the cat, Max the dog, Dottie the cat, Panda the cat, and Tony the fish.

ABOUT THE AUTHOR

Karen Wickerson has been an animal telepath/psychic/communicator since she was three years old and is a Healing Touch for Animals Certified Practitioner. *Listen to Your Animals: They Know More Than You Think* is her first book, and most likely won't be her last, although she'd like to think it is because she doesn't consider herself a writer. In fact, she finds it kind of painful.

In a previous part of life, she was a Clinical Family Counselor and holds a Master of Arts degree in Applied Behavioral Science. She hung up her counselor's hat to devote her life to and giving animals a voice and making a difference in their lives and the lives of their humans.

When she's not working with animals and their humans, she works closely with her alma mater, Trent University in Peterborough, Ontario, as their Westcoast Trent Chapter Chairperson and serves on their Philanthropic Advisory Committee.

She currently lives and plays in North Vancouver, British Columbia with her husband, Drummond, their two cats, Curious and Tenderfoot. She also loves spending time with her three granddaughters while excitedly waiting for her fourth's arrival in the new year.

To book a session with Karen or learn more about her and her offerings, visit karenwickerson.com. Or follow her on Instagram @karenwickersonanimaltelepath to stay informed of upcoming events and workshops.

www.ingramcontent.com/pod-product-compliance
Lightning Source LLC
Chambersburg PA
CBHW032026050726
47590CB00006B/2322